D0619886

Old Brooklyn Heights

NEW YORK'S FIRST SUBURB

Including Detailed Analyses of
619 Century-Old Houses

by

Clay Lancaster

Second Edition, With a Supplement
of New Photographs by

EDMUND V. GILLON, Jr.

DOVER PUBLICATIONS, INC.
NEW YORK

to

JAMES GROTE VAN DERPOOL

Former Professor of Architecture
at Columbia University
Avery Librarian
and First Executive Director
of the New York Landmarks Commission

This Dover Edition Is
Respectfully Dedicated

Frontispiece. No. 3 Monroe Place. (Photograph by Edmund V. Gillon, Jr.)

Published in Canada by General Publishing Company, Ltd., 30 Lesmill Road, Don Mills, Toronto, Ontario.
Published in the United Kingdom by Constable and Company, Ltd., 10 Orange Street, London WC2H 7EG.

This Dover edition, first published in 1979, is a corrected republication of the fifth (1969) printing of the work originally published by Charles E. Tuttle Company, Publishers, Rutland, Vermont & Tokyo, Japan, in 1961. The new foreword has been written especially for the Dover edition and a new supplement of photographs by Edmund V. Gillon, Jr., has been added. Several text photographs have also been replaced by new ones by Mr. Gillon.

International Standard Book Number:
0-486-23872-5
Library of Congress Catalog Card Number:
77-082191

Manufactured in the United States of America
Dover Publications, Inc.
180 Varick Street
New York, N. Y. 10014

Table of Contents

Foreword to the Dover Edition

How Brooklyn Heights Came To Be New York City's First Historic District

Iron fire escapes still disfigure some of the fine old row houses of brick and brownstone on Columbia Heights, Remsen Street and elsewhere in Brooklyn Heights, testifying to a period when the neighborhood, once a leading private-residential district of New York in the middle of the nineteenth century, had deteriorated into a section made up largely of rooming houses in the early twentieth century. An influx of new Americans, many of them speaking little or no English, some living in crowded, dingy conditions, flooded the area. Groceries and inns provided exotic offerings for the various ethnic groups. There was an international Y.M.C.A., and spotted about were missions, seamen's clubs, merchants' associations, and a foreign historical society—all serving Asians, Africans and Europeans. There were some undesirable establishments, but several venerable cultural institutions, such as Packer Collegiate Institute (on Joralemon Street since 1854) and the Long Island Historical Society (on Pierrepont Street since 1881), and a number of churches—Congregational, Presbyterian, Lutheran, Episcopal and Roman Catholic (most of them dating from the mid 1800s)—persevered, many of them with unabated vitality. A segment of the old-guard inhabitants also remained. In 1910 they founded two worthy organizations that were to do much toward reviving the Heights: the Brooklyn Heights Association and the Junior League. Each, in its own way, expanded the cultural horizons of adults and children.

Though it had been somewhat spoiled, Brooklyn Heights stood out as an architectural phenomenon in New York City. Its buildings largely belonged to the half century following the mechanization of the Fulton Street Ferry in 1814, and most of them remained standing. The region retains early-nineteenth-century charm and a quiet atmosphere, it is close to the commercial nucleus of the metropolis (connected by subway to Manhattan since 1910), so it was only natural that it should be rediscovered by people appreciative of its assets. They were mainly young married couples on the professional level—lawyers, architects, writers, teachers, etc.—whose awareness of the neighborhood nurtured the seeds of the idea that they should act to obtain official preservation of its amenities. If the Brooklyn Heights area is worthy of attention as a cultural monument, so is the process by which it attained the distinction of becoming New York's first historic district. The tale makes an interesting and valuable document that may serve as guide to inhabitants of other places having similar characteristics.

The spark that ignited the tinder was touched off by a young lawyer, Otis Pratt Pearsall, who, with his wife Nancy, was living in the basement apartment of a residence on Willow Street. On an evening late in the summer of 1958, John R. H. (Jack) Blum, another young lawyer and a summer bachelor, visited the Pearsalls. Jack Blum's family were long-time residents (and benefactors) of Brooklyn, and he recently had purchased one of the fine brownstones on Columbia Heights. Otis's ancestors had lived on Brooklyn Heights, and he and Nancy were hopeful of becoming householders in the community. Little did they realize how much time and work they would be involved in during the next six years, or the irony of how much more expensive they were making the realization of their dream of owning a house. In recalling that evening with Blum, Otis says:

> We shared a common enthusiasm for the area, and eventually our conversation turned to what might be done to assure the preservation of its charm. The immediate reasons for our concern were threefold. Only two years before, five houses had been torn down immediately next door to the house where we resided to make way for an ugly apartment building at 135 Willow Street. The Watchtower Society's plan to demolish several more houses along Willow and Orange Streets had just been disclosed. And Robert Moses' Slum Clearance Committee was preparing to swallow up the entire northeast corner of the Heights through the Cadman Plaza project. Jack, Nancy and I talked about the possibilities of some form of zoning to protect the Heights, and although I am not sure whether the Beacon Hill [Boston] example was specifically mentioned, I have always recalled this evening's discussion as the beginning point of my interest in Brooklyn Heights preservation.

Fortunately, two of Otis Pearsall's chief characteristics are perseverance and a passion for documentation. The one launched and sustained the program that is about to be outlined; the other provided the file materials used to compile this introduction. Nancy Pearsall shares these characteristics and helped greatly in the ensuing struggle.

In the following weeks a group of recent arrivals on the Heights began to coalesce to discuss ways and means for achieving the common cause. Among them were Martin Schneider, Malcolm Chesney and Arthur Steinberg. They called themselves the Community Conservation and Improvement Council, usually shortened to the initials CCIC (pronounced "kick"). Informal talks were held with New York housing officials and plans devised. By midwinter CCIC felt iself ready for public recognition and expansion.

An open meeting to present a statement of objectives, solicit adherents, elect officers and plan the work of committees was held on December 23 in the undercroft of the First Unitarian Church at Pierrepont Street and Monroe Place. A printed leaflet that was given out defined the neighborhood area as being north of Atlantic Avenue and between Court and Fulton streets and the East River. It announced that CCIC favored the minimum of demolition and relocation of Heights' residents, and recommended that the proposed Cadman Plaza project be slanted toward family housing, providing apartments of several bedrooms rather than single-occupancy efficiencies. Elected as cochairmen were Otis Pearsall, Martin Schneider and William R. Fisher. The last was another young lawyer, who headed the Brooklyn Heights Association's Housing Committee, which had a purpose similar to that of the new group. There was talk of merging the Committee and the Council, but the former detected in the latter a note of radicalism that it might not be able to endorse, and the latter feared its activities might be somewhat suppressed by the former. For the time being they kept their separate ways, though it was understood that they would work together, pooling their resources and their manpower for the good cause.

An article in the 1 January 1959 issue of the *Brooklyn Heights Press* stated CCIC's concern over current and pending destruction of buildings on the Heights. "Upon completion of demolition which even now rolls on," it said, "Willow Street alone will have lost nine houses in half as many years. If rumor becomes reality, more good houses, this time on Monroe Place, will soon be gone." The Willow Street loss had been caused by the construction of the apartment building at 135 and by the construction, then under way, of the Watchtower Society's residential hall for members of Jehovah's Witnesses. The demolition slated for Monroe Place was part of the Cadman Plaza expansion. On the positive side, in the same article, was the first published proposal for historic zoning of Brooklyn Heights: "Our houses, historic structures and the architectural character of the Heights must be rigidly preserved and safeguards must be developed to this end."

Means of attaining historic zoning were investigated. Correspondence was initiated with other groups involved in the same sort of endeavor, and various types of literature on the subject were collected. In late February Otis Pearsall wrote letters to the head of the Regional Plan Association and president of the Municipal Art Society requesting support for CCIC's case. In response, the Municipal Art Society established a special subcommittee of Alan Burnham's existing Committee on Historic Architecture. The offshoot designated to assist in the Brooklyn Heights program was made up of a worthy roster, including Burnham, Henry Hope Reed and the distinguished Albert S. Bard, a city planner then in his early nineties, after whom the Bard Law, a statute adopted by the state in 1956, had been named. The law authorized cities and towns to enact local preservation ordinances and opened the door to the sort of protection needed on the Heights.

At this stage the proposal for historic zoning of Brooklyn Heights was transformed from a dream to an actual working process. The first milestone was reached on 26 February 1959, at a meeting between the CCIC leadership and the Brooklyn Heights Association's Special Housing Committee to adopt a joint campaign. It was held at the Association headquarters on Montague Street. Otis Pearsall presented a program that included proposals for the preparation of an appropriate ordinance, the compilation of a survey of ante-bellum structures on the Heights, supplying proof of the worthiness of the cause, and the establishment of relations with allied parties (with or without official status) and with residents of the Heights. Arden Rathkopf, a lawyer and author of a leading treatise on zoning, and a governor of the Brooklyn Heights Association who had been working on a preservation program for the Association since 1957, was one of those present at the meeting. He was to make a valuable contribution to the effort in the days that followed. There were also

S. J. Schulman, the head of Westchester County's Planning Department, who attended under sponsorship of the Brooklyn Heights Association, Herbert Kaufman, head of the CCIC committee dealing with the Cadman Plaza project, Ted Reid, head of CCIC's Conservation Committee, and Arthur Hooker, head of its Ordinance Committee, and the CCIC cochairmen. Despite the differences of viewpoint between the two groups, the meeting ended in general agreement on the Pearsall plan.

The amalgamation of forces was made urgent when James Felt, Chairman of the New York City Planning Commission, proposed new city-wide zoning resolutions, which had been devised by a firm of consulting engineers. Hearings were to commence in the spring, and this seemed to be an opportune moment to present the Heights plan. Rathkopf, Schulman and Hooker were entrusted with the preparation of a draft amendment sympathetic to the zoning regulations. On 5 March 1959, *Brooklyn Heights Press* editor Richard Margolis, a steady supporter of the cause, presented an editorial entitled "How to Make History." He characterized the joint effort of the two local groups as beholden to the Bard Law and made an attractive public appeal: "If accepted by the City Planning Commission and the Board of Estimate, historic zoning would virtually guarantee stability on the Heights. The community would be free of all the predatory monsters that traditionally devour a neighborhood—the crowded rooming houses, the super-block high-income developments, the institutional dormitories."

The second item in Pearsall's plan, calling for a detailed survey of Brooklyn Heights architecture, was followed up by his meeting with Alan Burnham, and in discussions with Wayne Andrews, Henry Hope Reed and Miss Maud Esther Dilliard, all of whom were writers and lecturers on historic architecture; the last two also being contributors to the *New York Landmarks,* a survey compiled for the Municipal Art Society during the 1950s. They all recommended Clay

Lancaster, a former teacher in the Department of Fine Arts at Columbia University and Cooper Union, a lecturer in the Metropolitan Museum of Art, and a specialist in American architecture, as a person qualified to undertake such a survey. Lancaster, then pursuing an independent career as a writer, was a Heights resident. He responded to their proposal with enthusiasm; it was arranged that a sum to defray expenses would be made available from the Robert E. Blum Foundation through the Long Island Historical Society which, by this time, had pledged allegiance to the movement through its president, Edgarton G. North. The survey was begun immediately, tabulating each house by style, period and physical characteristics. Later the work was amplified by documentation on each building, a description of streets, a discussion of the architectural development, and with the addition of illustrations it became the book here being reprinted.

Clay Lancaster's initial survey took several months to compile and was not ready for the zoning ordinance hearing held on 13 April 1959. The proposal presented by Arden Rathkopf on behalf of the Brooklyn Heights Association was of a general nature, favoring the creation of historic districts throughout the city. Although backed by Ted Reid as spokesman for CCIC, in its lack of specific benefits for Brooklyn Heights the proposal fell far short of what the Community Conservation and Improvement Council had in mind. The group felt called upon to act on its own.

CCIC staged a forum on April 21 in the Gold Room of the Bossert Hotel. Donald W. McKinney, minister of the First Unitarian Church, was chairman of the meeting, and guest speaker was State Senator MacNeil Mitchell, coauthor of the Mitchell-Lama Law (favoring middle-income housing). During the meeting Martin Schneider read a letter sent by CCIC to Robert Moses, chairman of the city's Slum Clearance Committee, urging him to accept the council's plan for middle-income cooperatives on Cadman Plaza and the inclusion of a new public school on Clark Street. The letter sought to amend the existing tendency to ignore the character of the Heights, which would make it virtually "a backdrop of the civic center." Otis Pearsall gave a speech in which he spelled out why Brooklyn Heights needed historic zoning, what it was, and how CCIC meant to go about attaining it. William Hall of CCIC's General Planning Committee showed slides of Brooklyn Heights maps indicating the condition of residential buildings (rated good, fair, poor, and bad), the kinds of buildings (single- or multiple-family dwellings, commercial, etc.), those that were owner-occupied, and transportation facilities. The CCIC program was applauded by its ally, the Brooklyn Heights Association, and by the Democrats of the Third Assembly District, the West Brooklyn Independent Democrats, and the South Brooklyn Neighborhood Houses. It was significant that the forum was attended by a record crowd of about 400 Heights residents, and that its proceedings were covered by the *New York Times,* the *World-Telegram* and the National Broadcasting Company. CCIC's voice was being heard far afield.

Many years later Otis Pearsall wrote of the forum at the Bossert:

> In retrospect this town meeting, which was a major step in the downfall of Moses' Slum Clearance Committee, represented CCIC's zenith. At the BHA annual meeting the following month Schneider, Chesney, Hooker and Reid were all elected to the BHA Board. The election of such a large part of the CCIC leadership to the BHA Board eventually and quite predictably crippled CCIC. Martin Schneider and Malcolm Chesney continued the Cadman Plaza fight under both the BHA and CCIC banners. Ted Reid became Chairman of the BHA Civic Improvement Committee and, so far as I know, never again was involved with historic zoning. Arthur Hooker became Chairman of the BHA Housing Violations Committee, and this superseded his work on the historic zoning ordinance. For my part, I had in January 1959 taken a leave of absence from my law firm to join the United States Attorney's Office for the Southern District of New York. With the advent of

> summer and the increasing pressures of my new job, I had diminishing time to devote to CCIC and, in fact, resigned as Co-Chairman in the fall of 1959. CCIC for all practical purposes was absorbed into the BHA by the end of 1959 and, although Ken Boss [a realtor on Montague Street and resident in the Heights] and a few of his colleagues continued to utilize the CCIC name for at least a year or two longer, the remarkable spontaneous experiment it represented expired just about a year after it began.

In the April 23 issue of the *Brooklyn Heights Press* appeared the first of six articles by Clay Lancaster on the major styles of period architecture represented on the Heights. On the evening of 17 February 1960 the material was presented in toto as a talk with colored slides. It was sponsored by the Junior League in the undercroft of the First Unitarian Church and bore the title that was to appear on the author's forthcoming book, "Old Brooklyn Heights: New York's First Suburb." The lecture was given to an overflow audience, and it was repeated at the Long Island Historical Society on March 3 at the Brooklyn Museum on March 27 at the Friends' School on April 14 and at the Pierrepont Tuesday Club on May 24. The talk was performed many times again both in and out of New York during the next decade.

Phase Two of the endeavor to attain historic zoning for Brooklyn Heights began with the Brooklyn Heights Association's Golden Jubilee, which was open to the public, in the spring of 1960. Joining the Association in the festivities were its contemporary, the Junior League, and its older ally the Long Island Historical Society. The latter put on a special exhibition, "The Brooklyn Heights Story," assembled by Miss Maud Dilliard. It consisted of maps, prints and photographs pertaining to the area from early Dutch times to its heyday in the late nineteenth century. The Golden Jubilee itself was inaugurated on April 19 by a Festival of Flowers arranged by the Brooklyn Heights Garden Club at the Grace Church parish house. On April 23 there was a Jubilee Garden Sale on Willow Place under the joint auspices of the Garden Club and the Willowtown Association. Brooklyn Heights Week started officially on May 2 by proclamation of Borough President John Cashmore. The *Brooklyn Heights Press* published a special commemorative issue edited by Rita Bird and Lyle Smith, with contributions by Peggy Zorach, Tessim Zorach, William A. Hall, Georgene Maxwell, Mary Lou Fisher, Richard Margolis, and Otis Pearsall; it also included a photograph contest on Heights subjects. An exhibition of paintings, sculpture, and graphics was given at the Casino Club, and three one-act plays were presented at the First Unitarian Church over the weekend of May 7-8. The culminating event transpired at the Hotel St. George on Monday evening, May 9. At 8:00 P.M. the winning photographs of the camera competition and an historical exhibition were displayed in the outer galleries, and at 8:30 a business meeting assembled in the Grand Ballroom. William Fisher presided over the special program that followed. Guest speaker was Richard H. Howland, President of the National Trust for Historic Preservation in Washington, D.C., who outlined the characteristics and advantages of historic zoning legislation. An announcement of the Association's proposed historic-zoning ordinance was made by the Hon. Leonard P. Moore, Judge of the U.S. Court of Appeals and a Heights resident. The meeting concluded with an informal consultation between those attending, members of the Association's various committees, and those in charge of the anteroom exhibitions. Over 700 persons attended.

The success of the jubilee meeting prompted the next step, which was taken by the Board of Governors of the Brooklyn Heights Association five weeks later. President William Fisher proposed that a new committee be formed to establish foundations for historic zoning of the Heights. Otis Pearsall, who had been elected to the Board on May 9, underscored the proposal by stating that this undoubtedly would be the society's most important project over the next few years, and he suggested that it be patterned on the first of such endeavors, at Beacon Hill, Boston. Edgarton North was named chairman, and committee members, elected over several months, were Fisher, Pearsall, Judge Leonard Moore, Clay Lancaster, Houghton H. Bell, and Roy Richardson. The committee had a long and useful history. In 1962, North, Fisher, and Pearsall acted as cochairmen, and a year later the last two shared the reins.

In October Otis Pearsall presented to the Association what he called the "Battle Plan for the Preservation of Brooklyn Heights." He pointed out that of the two foremost candidates for neighborhood historic protection in New York City, the Heights had considerable superiority over Greenwich Village. The plan called for a system of subcommittees to deal with the various facets of the project—exploring its possibilities, devising a proper statute, financing, and establishing good relations with groups and individuals. Choosing the right person to officiate in each capacity was the work of a number of months, and by March, 1961, there were 42 working members besides the original 7 on the parent committee. Special notice is due Richard Lange, chairman of the Site Committee, for his work on the maps reflecting the changing ideas regarding the proper boundaries for the historic district, including the final version that was awarded landmark status several years later.

Outrider to the next milestone in the Brooklyn Heights journey toward preservation was an article by Brooks Atkinson in his "Critic at Large" series in the *New York Times* on 2 May 1961. Atkinson presented the view that the Cadman Plaza development, by erecting monstrous luxury and cooperative high-rise buildings, would upset the scale of Brooklyn Heights. He took his cue from "an excellent brochure on the subject" edited by Martin S. James, Assistant Professor of Art at Brooklyn College. With Eric Salzman, James was a leader in the North Heights Community Group, which had banded together to oppose expansion of the Cadman Plaza threat into their territory. Atkinson described the small houses that prompt a friendly and neighborly existence, where "children have a normal life in the gardens, on the stoops or in and out of the houses. The residents do not want this style of living replaced by what Professor James calls 'a dead-level apartment world, a one-class residential dormitory.'" Where possible, renovation is to be preferred to wholesale destruction of old buildings to retain human scale.

Within a fortnight of publication of the article the 51st annual meeting of the Brooklyn Heights Association was held. Guest speaker was John Codman, who had been instrumental in getting preservation legislation for Beacon Hill five years earlier. Codman, a realtor, held a meeting with Heights people involved in real estate in the afternoon, before the evening general assembly. He pointed out the advantages to them of historic zoning, which gives aesthetic and permanent stabilization to a neighborhood and keeps property values high. His talk on the evening of May 15 in the Grand Ballroom of the St. George Hotel offered two encouraging points concerning the Heights: it was the outstanding community in New York City for claiming the benefits of historic zoning; inasmuch as its existing structures could be economically maintained for contemporary use, landmark status was not naive or visionary but sound, realistic and workable. He rededicated his listeners to the cause of safeguarding their rich architectural heritage for posterity.

In introducing Codman, Otis Pearsall offered some rousing remarks in favor of neighborhood preservation, and in recording the St. George meeting in the report of the Brooklyn Heights Association he headed his paragraph "Annual Meeting Initiates Historic Zoning Drive." In effect it introduced Phase Three of the movement, which lasted the summer of 1962. During it a number of tangible strides forward were made.

The first was the framing of an acceptable zoning statute. The rough draft was begun by Allan McGrath as chairman of the Statute Committee. Unfortunately, the pressure of McGrath's law practice hindered him from taking the matter further. The standard was taken up by Otis Pearsall, who compared the McGrath effort with ten or twelve working statutes around the country. He then devised a document that was virtually an amendment to the Zoning Resolution of the City of New York, in the form of an Article VIII, establishing the district of Old Brooklyn Heights. It was typed and circulated among the committee, and after a few minor changes suggested by Burton White action was ready to be taken on it.

Further interest in the Heights was precipitated by two tours during the fall of 1961. The first, on September 10 was led by Henry Hope Reed as one in his Sunday walking tours given under the auspices of the Museum of the City of New York. The other walk, on Sunday, October 15, was programed as part of the annual meeting of the National Trust for Historic Preservation in New York City. Participants in both were furnished with printed notes on the architecture viewed taken from Clay Lancaster's forthcoming *Old Brooklyn Heights*. Lancaster assisted Reed as tour leader; he and Otis Pearsall guided the Washington group.

Old Brooklyn Heights itself, published by the Charles E. Tuttle Co. of Rutland, Vermont, and Tokyo, Japan, made its appearance in December. Through announcements to members of the Brooklyn Heights Association and Long Island Historical Society over 750 copies were sold on a prepublication offer; the book then was distributed through bookstores. The *New York Times* presented an illustrated review of the book and preservation movement on the Heights written by Martin Arnold on 9 December 1961. The Municipal Art Society awarded the book a citation at City Hall the following May 15. The Tuttle edition of *Old Brooklyn Heights* went through five printings, the last coming out in 1969.

In October 1961, armed with an advance copy of the book and several of the large colored maps the production of which had been keeping pace with other aspects of the project, Otis Pearsall and

Edgarton North met with James Felt of the City Planning Commission. The interview showed Felt that Brooklyn Heights had done its homework well, that it was unquestionably deserving of historic preservation and that, being threatened, it was urgently in need of historic-zoning protection. Felt referred the representatives from the Heights to the Committee for the Preservation of Structures of Historic and Esthetic Importance, which he had urged Mayor Robert Wagner to appoint the previous summer. The committee was composed of thirteen members, headed by Geoffrey Platt and including Harmon H. Goldstone, both of whom headed the later Landmarks Commission in succession.

A meeting between Platt and Goldstone and the Heights Association team was arranged by Mrs. Darwin James, one of Goldstone's fellow board members on the Municipal Art Society, at her home on Pierrepont Place. At its conclusion there was a hurried tour of the neighborhood. At a follow-up meeting at Platt's architectural office on December 12, Pearsall presented maps and statistics. Goldstone was considerably more enthusiastic over the Heights project than Platt, who seemed reluctant to deal with the area separately from the city. However, Platt consistently testified to the Heights' claim to preservation priority in the press.

In March of 1962 the Brooklyn Heights Association and the Long Island Historical Society hosted a luncheon attended by key local and government officials involved in preservation. Among them were Congressman (later Governor) Hugh Carey, Borough Historian James Kelley, Dr. Charles W. Porter III, and Dr. Thomas Pitkin of the National Park Service.

The Brooklyn Heights effort came to a climax on 30 April 1962, when a copy of the preservation proposal, including the suggested statute, a map of the historic district, a revised set of the data and style statistics, and a current press release, was sent to the mayor and every city and federal official in any way concerned. The press release contained not only an eloquent advocacy for, but considerable information about, the proposition. It was given good coverage in the *Herald Tribune, World Telegram* and the *Mirror*. The *Tribune* article reported Geoffrey Platt as saying that Brooklyn Heights "should have first priority in any effort to preserve what is left of old New York."

Immediately thereafter a battery of block captains was organized to explain the proposal to property holders and residents, and to obtain signatures on a supporting petition. This brought about 50 persons actively into the enterprise. They were given printed sheets of instructions and information, and by the end of the summer well over one-third of the owners and over 2000 others had affixed their signatures to the document. The popular enthusiasm engendered was heartening.

The annual meeting of the Brooklyn Heights Association, held on the evening of 14 May 1962 in the ballroom of the St. George, offered a substantial display of articles and visual materials by the Historic Preservation Committee. At the assembly Otis Pearsall warned of the destruction that would occur if the ordinance did not become a reality. Guest speaker was Congressman Hugh Carey. He noted in his talk that federal officials, who had recently visited the Heights at his invitation, agreed unanimously that it was the outstanding area for historic preservation in New York City, and that it had, in principle, the support of them all.

The first of two significant events in the summer of 1962 was a panel discussion on preservation sponsored by the West Brooklyn Independent Democrats. It resulted in considerable and generally positive publicity. The second, and the more important in having a bearing upon the Heights situation, was a panel discussion between Otis Pearsall, James Felt and three others on WCBS-TV's "New

York Forum" on August 12. In the spring Mayor Wagner had replaced Platt's Committee for the Preservation of Structures by the twelve-member Landmarks Preservation Commission with Platt as chairman. The change from a committee to a commission seemed more authoritative and Pearsall took the opportunity to sound out Felt (as chairman of the City Planning Commission) on how prospects seemed for getting immediate historic zoning. James Felt reiterated his support of the project but said that it would have to wait and be included in a citywide program to be developed by the Landmarks Preservation Commission. It now was clear from what source the favor was to emanate, yet further patience would have to be exercised before it was to become a reality.

A minor fight, waged at this time as part of the general opposition against the pending Cadman Plaza project, centered on the building at the south corner of Cranberry and Fulton Streets. It had housed the printing office of the Rome brothers, publishers of Walt Whitman's *Leaves of Grass*. Elias S. Wilentz, proprietor of the Eighth Street Bookshop in Greenwich Village and a home owner on Middagh Street, head of the Committee to Save the Walt Whitman Building, had assembled enthusiastic statements from America's living literary giants, among them Robert Frost, Carl Sandburg, Marianne Moore, and Arthur Miller, attesting to the cultural significance of the building. It qualified for four out of the six points listed by the Department of the Interior for inclusion on the National Register of Historic Places yet was turned down. It was demolished along with all other centenarian buildings in the stretch along Fulton Street two years later.

Phase Four of the preservation movement began in October 1962 when Mayor Wagner appointed William R. Fisher to the Landmarks Preservation Commission through the good offices of Hugh Carey. With one of its most able enthusiasts on the Commission, the Heights had a definite advantage. It was informed of developments directly and had means of expressing its ideas and views to the Commission firsthand.

In December the Brooklyn Heights Association announced the establishment of a Design Advisory Council, headed by Edwards Rullman, which included George P. Howard, Ralph F. Cameron, William Hall, Herbert Kaufman, Joseph Merz (all architects living on the Heights), and Fisher, Pearsall, and Lancaster. The purpose of the Design Advisory Council was to give free architectural guidance on local buildings, especially as regards their preservation and restoration. It also was empowered to issue bronze date plaques for homeowners who wanted to publicize the age of their houses. The volunteer group served a useful purpose in heading off much unnecessary defacement and destruction of Brooklyn Heights architecture while waiting for the City to launch its program.

Early in 1963 the Landmarks Preservation Commission drafted a measure to put before the City Planning Commission. James Grote Van Derpool, for some years Professor of Architecture at Columbia University and Avery Librarian, was the first executive director of the Landmarks Commission. An article by Thomas W. Ennis in the *New York Times* on July 21 announced that the commission had tentatively designated 300 buildings, a number of bridges and monuments and the districts of Greenwich Village and Brooklyn Heights as worthy of preservation. For a neighborhood to qualify for this honor 65 percent of its buildings had to contain "historic interest." Matters proceeded slowly, and it was not until 5 October 1964 that a bill to preserve the city's architectural heritage was introduced into the City Council. The commission by that time had selected 4423 individual structures worthy of preservation, of which Greenwich Village accounted for 2967, Brooklyn Heights 1192 and a cast-iron district in the vicinity of Greene Street and Broadway 50. Owners of designated buildings who could establish inability to earn a reasonable return on the property might apply to the commission for relief, which could take the form of tax exemption or tax remission. A month later a special meeting was held at the Hillis Hall building of the Plymouth Church of the Pilgrims in Brooklyn to brief Heights residents on what the proposed law would mean to the community. Otis Pearsall was master of ceremonies, and speakers included Geoffrey Platt, William Fisher, Edwards Rullman and Clay Lancaster.

An unusual and venturesome endeavor that was an offshoot of the movement on the Heights was the rescue of various architectural features from historic buildings slated for demolition in the Cadman Plaza area. In 1963 Clay Lancaster made arrangements to salvage the fine iron front fence and second-story balcony on 97 Clark Street, an early 1830s residence and former home of Paul Leicester Ford, for reuse in restoring the P. C. Cornell house at 108 Pierrepont Street, which dated from the same period. This was an ill-fated project, but part of the fence ended up in the sculpture garden of the Brooklyn Museum and the balcony on 157 Columbia Heights. The main thrust of salvaging was conducted by two teams on 21 March 1964. Led by Lancaster and Pearsall, they had the able support of Edwards Rullman, Martin Schneider, Richard Lange, Mrs. Nancy Pearsall, Mrs. Carol Howard and Mrs. Mary Lou Fisher. The teams entered all of the old buildings likely to yield treasures and earmarked Federal and Greek Revival marble and wood mantels, a scroll-shaped mahogany newel post and other woodwork, and a three-story circular stairway with wrought-iron post and railing. C. R. Jones, a graduate student at the Institute of Fine Arts of New York University and an inveterate collector of relics, was put in charge of dismantling about thirty finds. They were put on display and sold in the lower story of the Long Island Historical Society building on May 2. Prices ranged from $2 for an iron fireplace summer front to $100 for a marble chimneypiece. The stairway and newel post were disposed of on a bid basis. Proceeds were used to defray acquisition expenses and to further the work of the Historic Preservation Committee of the Brooklyn Heights Association.

On 3 December 1964 the Committee on Codification of the New York City Council held a hearing on the Landmarks Preservation statute. It was arranged for each member of the committee to receive a copy of *Old Brooklyn Heights;* and it was appropriate that the prime mover and indefatigable worker for the cause, Otis Pratt Pearsall, cochairman of the Historic Preservation Committee, should represent the Brooklyn Heights Association and make a speech on behalf of the proposal. It was the climax of his many good speeches given on the subject over the previous five years. After stating that the enactment of the statute had the backing of the Heights Association's 1200 members and of several thousand Heights residents (as shown by the petition signed in 1962), Pearsall pointed out that Brooklyn Heights, "saved by the East River from the development experienced by similar areas in downtown Manhattan, and left behind as Brooklyn expanded out into its open areas," was "the finest remaining microcosm of our City as it looked more than 100 years ago." He named the two foremost enemies to maintaining the status quo of the area: demolition of historic buildings for erecting apartments; defacement of existing structures through ill-conceived renovations. The proposed landmarks preservation bill would curb these two evils. The Brooklyn Heights Association issued the whole of the Pearsall speech in its December *Bulletin* to the members.

While awaiting the city's decision on the matter, Brooklyn Heights was declared an Historic District by the Department of the Interior, as announced by the Hon. Stewart L. Udall, Secretary, on 13 January 1965. It was the culmination of a sustained effort on the part of Hugh Carey, William Fisher and others of the Historic Preservation Committee, whereby Brooklyn Heights was listed on the National Register of Historic Places. It was an honor which had been denied the Walt Whitman building and which had been awarded to Plymouth Church in 1962. A bronze marker bestowed upon the Heights was attached to a base designed and executed by James DeMartis and Nat LaPadura, representing the early Pierrepont mansion, Four Chimneys. It was placed in the lower terrace of the Long Island Historical Society building at the corner of Pierrepont and Clinton streets.

On 6 April 1965 the City Council unanimously approved the Landmarks Preservation Law. On April 19 the Brooklyn Heights Association issued a press release by George Howard, recounting the history of the preservation effort. The law was signed by Mayor Wagner on the same day. At this stage the Brooklyn Heights enthusiasts had contributed substantially to getting a bill passed for the potential benefit of historic monuments throughout the city yet had achieved nothing tangible for their own prime interest. Their goal still lay some months away.

The final lap of the race constitutes Phase Five. This period was not spent waiting idly for the inevitable; the struggle continued unabated. Every aspect of the claim for historic preservation of Brooklyn Heights was challenged. For one, the question was raised whether Cobble Hill should be included in the proposed district. Upon looking into the matter it was seen that the area to the south was totally unprepared to make any kind of a presentation in the foreseeable future, and it was decided by the Landmarks Commission that it must wait its turn. Work on the neighborhood map had to be brought up to final form, and now included the north side of Atlantic Avenue from the Brooklyn-Queens Expressway on the west to a little short of Court Street on the east, north to Joralemon Street, west to Clinton Street, north to beyond Pierrepont Street (with an eastward jog to take in Spencer Memorial Church), then to include both sides of Monroe Place north to Clark Street (omitting the Church of the Restoration site on the corner), westward to Hicks Street and then back Pineapple to Henry (eliminating the St. George complex), northward to Middagh Street, westward to Hicks, north to Poplar, and thence back to the beginning following the Brooklyn-Queens Expressway or Promenade over it. The other Herculean task, which fell mostly on the shoulders of Mrs. Nancy Pearsall, was compiling a card file to include each of the 1316 lots within the proposed district. *Old Brooklyn Heights* had included notes on only 619 pre-Civil War houses still serving residential purposes, plus a handful of important public buildings included in the discussions on the streets, but there were still as many more to be done.

Eventually, on November 1 the Landmarks Commission published its proposal for naming Brooklyn Heights an Historic District. A public hearing was held at City Hall on November 17. Otis Pearsall and some 40 others spoke in favor of the designation. Nobody appeared in opposition, though representatives of the Watchtower Society and St. Francis College asked that their properties be excluded from the proposed territory. The institutional requests were not heeded when the historic district designation was promulgated on 23 November 1965. It was two days before Thanksgiving, which is remembered on Brooklyn Heights as a day warranting something truly to be grateful for. The territory indicated was that described in the preceding paragraph, except that the St. George Hotel block and the northern tip of the Heights were included. A map showing the district appears on pages 164 and 165. Shortly thereafter the Board of Estimate confirmed the Commission's designation, which was the final step in that long uphill struggle.

Brooklyn Heights had won the battle, but the question remained whether it had won the war. The landmarks law as enacted contained several weaknesses. One of major consequence was that demolition of desirable buildings remained possible where an owner could demonstrate inability to achieve a certain rate of return on his property and where the city was unwilling either to condemn or grant tax abatement on it. Another was that a new structure could be erected out of scale relationship to its environment. The latter was considered a traditional zoning concern, but that it should be a matter for the Landmarks Commission soon became apparent when it became known that the Watchtower Society was contemplating a 12-story building on Columbia Heights between Clark and Pineapple streets. Prompted by the fact that buildings below the Promenade were restricted by a height limitation to preserve the famous view, it seemed logical that those atop the bluff could also be limited for an esthetic reason. The matter was taken up with Beverly Spatt, who was then on the City Planning Commission. At her suggestion it was presented in the form of a letter from the Brooklyn Heights Association to the Hon. William F. R. Ballard, chairman of the commission. The letter, dated 19 April 1966, requested an amendment to the City Zoning Resolution setting a 50-foot height restriction on all new buildings throughout an historic district, and it was signed by Francis J. H. De Rosa, chairman of the Zoning Committee, Otis Pratt Pearsall, cochairman of the Historic Preservation Committee, and Edwards F. Rullman, chairman of the Design Advisory Council.

Restricting the height of a building was a clever device for deterring developers from going to the expense of demolishing old structures simply for increasing income by increasing capacity. Eventually the City Planning Department Staff prepared the text of an acceptable amendment to the Zoning Resolution, which was given a hearing by the City Planning Commission on November 2. It was approved and reached the Board of Estimate for confirmation on December 22. Here it was strenuously opposed by the city's organized real estate industry, but through hard lobbying bolstered by a speech from Pearsall, the amendment was carried by a vote of 12 to 10. Once the amendment was adopted the next task was getting Brooklyn Heights designated as the first Limited Height District. The proposal was heard by the City Planning Commission on 7 June 1967 and was confirmed by the Board of Estimate on August 24. The new restriction was first used for a relatively happy settlement of the Watchtower Society's project. The result was a small modern building replacing the old Norwegian Club at the corner of Columbia Heights and Pineapple Street, and saving the facades of the three old brick row houses to the south.

It is regrettable that the preservation clamp was not tightened on Brooklyn Heights sooner. The old Pierrepont mansion by Richard Upjohn at 1 Pierrepont Place was demolished in 1946. Several blocks of the northwest corner of the Heights, razed for the construction of the Brooklyn-Queens Expressway in 1953, contained the interesting Long Island and Atlantic National Bank building on the north side of Fulton Street (opposite Hicks) and others in the row. By the beginning of 1954 the Renaissance Revival brownstone at 222 Columbia Heights (across from the site of the Pierrepont mansion) was undergoing demolition. The most lamentable losses were those dating from the early period of the preservation movement. Foremost was the King's County Courthouse, pictured on page 55, which, although outside Brooklyn Heights proper, keyed in with the historic district along with the neighboring City Hall (now Borough Hall). Also destroyed in 1960, to make way for the box-like new library branch, were the Venetian Gothic Brooklyn Mercantile Library on Montague Street (page 58) and the French Renaissance Hotel Touraine and adjoining domed Saracenic old Crescent Club (1891) on Clinton Street. In the same year the three Gothic Revival row brownstone houses, Nos. 118–122 Willow Street, were disfigured by an ill-conceived addition atop the southernmost, including a needless removal of the cornice. A new story was added to 27 Monroe Place, surmounting what already was a modern addition.

The manuscript of *Old Brooklyn Heights: New York's First Suburb* had already gone to the publisher and changes to the last-mentioned and succeeding items are not recorded in the book. Two houses that stood opposite Plymouth Church on Orange Street, Nos. 52 and 54 (page 123)—the latter a frame house dating from the 1820s—were torn down in 1961 to make room for an apartment house. At about the same time the thirteen adjoining rear yards with handsome *claire-voie* iron fence along Grace Court were spoiled when three were usurped for a nondescript multiple-housing unit, entailing the mutilation of the handsome elm tree in the court dating from before the American Revolution, upsetting its balance and contributing to its overthrow on 20 September 1977.

Insofar as wholesale destruction of historic monuments on Brooklyn Heights is concerned, the most devastating year was 1964. The northwest corner of the Heights lost to the Brooklyn-Queens Expressway eleven years earlier was but a fraction of the size of the entire east face from Pierrepont Street up to the expressway site that was razed at this time. Heading the list of casualties were the Brooklyn Savings Bank, one of four noteworthy buildings at the intersection of Pierrepont and Clinton streets (page 62), and the Church of the Restoration on Monroe Place (page 103). Private residences listed in this book which fell prey to the development were 29 and 89 Henry Street (page 101), 8 Monroe Place (page 105), 29–31 Clinton Street (pages 113, 115), and 91, 95 and 97 Clark Street (page 127). Also in 1964, despite the well-known push for preservation on the Heights, the original doors of the Spencer Memorial Church on Remsen Street were replaced by a different and less appropriate design. The following year Our Lady of Lebanon (page 96), originally the Church of the Pilgrims, outdid its neighbor by discarding its old wood doors and substituting ones of bronze embellished with plaques taken from the ocean liner *Normandie* that burned in the New York harbor in 1942.

In 1966, immediately following landmark designation, 108 Pierrepont Street, which had been in process of restoration for use as a private home (the bay window alongside the front door had been removed and replaced by a facsimile of the original opening), was taken over by a developer. The window sashes were supplanted by inappropriate models, and holes were cut through the walls for air conditioners. Ridiculously narrow shutters were hung on the windows, but a storm of neighborhood protest succeeded in getting them removed within a week.

In the summer of 1966 there was one notable restoration. The not-very-old box vestibule of 178 Columbia Heights was removed and a copy of its 1840 portico was replaced under the direction of Clay Lancaster and Edwards Rullman. Simultaneously the Watchtower Society was cooperating with preservationists two blocks to the north, as mentioned above.

Their fate sealed before the designation of the Heights as a landmark district, several late nineteenth-century houses on Remsen Street (page 140) were destroyed to enlarge St. Francis College. Vandalism occurring about this time included the theft of the bronze plaque awarded by the Department of the Interior from the areaway of the Long Island Historical Society, and the disappearance of one of the iron basket urns in front of 46 Monroe Place (page 104). In 1968 the frieze windows of 3 Pierrepont Place were cut down into the architrave—a defacement which remains.

On the brighter side, and the reward for all of the hours and effort that were poured into the cause for historic preservation, is the fact that no ante-bellum building has come down since St. Francis College took its toll. Restoration of frame houses has included 31–33 Middagh Street (clapboards replacing stucco) and 38–40 Hicks Street, all four of which had been in a dilapidated condition. The balcony on 157 Columbia Heights, taken from 97 Clark Street, has been mentioned. The doorway of 100 Hicks Street, inappropriate to the building's period, was replaced by one of the proper type. Leading missing from the transom and sidelights of 157 Willow Street was restored. Late in the year 1976 the stoops at 45 Sidney Place and 36 Pierrepont Street were brought back to their original form. As a parting remark on a happy note, Otis and Nancy Pearsall purchased one of the oldest and most charming houses on the Heights. They have spent many pleasant hours in its restoration and now occupy it with their young daughter.

*NOTE: Asterisks (*) have been added in the margin of this edition to denote buildings that have been razed since the original publication of the book in **1961**.*

Old Brooklyn Heights

"VIEW OF BROOKLYN, L.I., FROM U.S. HOTEL IN NEW YORK." Lithograph by E. Whitfield made in 1845. This detail of a wide panoramic view includes from the northernmost tip of Brooklyn Heights (Fulton Ferry, extreme left) beyond the south boundary of the Pierrepont estate. Hezekiah B. Pierrepont's 18th-century house, "Four Chimneys," may be seen among the trees above the bluff near the right margin of the picture. A trio of existing Heights churches built in 1844 are shown. These are Richard Upjohn's Church of the Pilgrims (first spire to the left of the Pierrepont house), Minard Lafever's Church of the Holy Trinity (tallest spire), and the same

architect's Unitarian Church of the Saviour (adjacent to Holy Trinity). The house with the round cupola (touching the corner of the Church of the Saviour) is the Leavitt-Bowen mansion that stood facing Columbia Heights on the north side of Clark Street until 1904. Underhill's Colonnade Row, on Columbia Heights between Middagh and Cranberry, is directly above the ferryboat leaving the New York slip—From a print belonging to the Pierreponts, now in the collection of Mr. and Mrs. M. Kenneth Boss. Reproduced through the courtesy of the present owners.

List of Illustrations

Unless otherwise credited in the accompanying captions, the drawings and photographs are by the author.

Preface

THIS IS a book about the old buildings of Brooklyn Heights, New York, featuring those that reckon their years of existence in three figures. Undoubtedly many persons living on the Heights will be—just as I was—surprised to learn that there are still standing over six hundred houses upwards of a century old. By actual count 619 of them are analyzed in the pages that follow. There are others, not included here because they lie on the insecure perimeter of Brooklyn Heights, or else because they have been converted, beyond the possibility of restoration, into places of business, such as on Montague Street. The area dealt with extends from Middagh to State streets, and from Columbia Heights to Henry Street as far south as Clark, and then takes in Monroe Place and the blocks below Joralemon over to Court Street. The detailed notes concentrate upon residential examples, but contemporary public buildings and later buildings of both kinds are discussed in the sections having to do with architectural styles, as well as in the street descriptions preceding the house listings.

The main purpose behind this study is to provide local residents and others with concrete information regarding the architectural heritage of Brooklyn Heights. Toward this end individual houses are written up in the form of notes. Obviously these notes cannot be read in the manner of a novel, seated in an easy armchair, and it is suggested that they will be most useful taken along on a Sunday afternoon walking tour, doing a few streets at a time. The make-up of these notes includes three parts: first, a description of each house as it looked originally, insofar as can be ascertained through available evidence, giving the number of stories, the material comprising the front wall (wood, brick, or stone), its architectural style if it be definite, and noteworthy details; second, some statistics about the house, its initial listing in a Brooklyn city directory, the house number(s) by which it was designated prior to the installation of the modern numbering system in 1871, and the name or names of its earliest inhabitants, some of which undoubtedly are those of tenants or boarders, or even of servants living on the premises; and third, an analysis of later alterations. Unless otherwise noted, brickwork referred to is of the unbonded, or all-stretcher variety, the use of Flemish bond and common bond in this community being the exception rather than the rule. For those unfamiliar with technical terms a glossary is provided at the end.

At this point a word should be in order about the method employed in carrying out the current project. It began with a study of the physical aspects of the various houses, notes being made of their characteristics. These results were compared with two invaluable documents, maps of the City of Brooklyn showing the outline of every building in existence (indicating by colors whether frame or masonry), produced by William Perris, civil engineer and surveyor, and published by Perris and Browne, New York, in 1855 and 1860. The contemporary street number for each house given on these two maps provided the search-list for looking up most of the houses in the Brooklyn city directories, that go back to 1822. Especially useful were the directories for the years 1840 and 1841, because they contain, in addition to the regular alphabetical inventory of residents found also in the others, a street-by-street guide, listing the names of persons living in consecutive houses. These proved most helpful for streets in the southern section of Brooklyn Heights, where house numbering was still in its infancy during the early eighteen forties. Searching for initial entries is a tedious and time-consuming chore, but it has been the means of obtaining the desired information, whereas going through the municipal records of Brooklyn would have been virtually an endless task.

As stated earlier, the present survey was undertaken to make available to Heights dwellers and others reliable data on the older houses in this neighborhood, not merely to satisfy whatever curiosity they may have about them, but with the hope of stimulating a deep-seated interest and regard for the high standards of craftsmanship found in old buildings that will be conducive to the preservation of them. The project of compiling such a work was first suggested to the author in April, 1959, by Mr. Otis Pratt Pearsall, then an officer of the Community Conservation and Improvement Council, a group banded together by the mutual objective of maintaining the traditional atmosphere of Brooklyn Heights. For the most part the members of this group were young married couples who had purchased buildings in the area, often those that were once proud residences which had deteriorated into overcrowded rooming houses, and had converted them back into private homes for normal family living. In general the talents of these young people now have been channeled into the work of other associations of similar purpose.

The author would like to take this opportunity to express his gratitude to the officers and members of the two long-established cultural organizations in this community, the Long Island Historical Society and the Brooklyn Heights Association, for their interest and help in his project. He is indebted especially to Mr. Pearsall, whose numerous suggestions proved extremely beneficial in its taking definitive shape, and to Mrs. Nancy Pearsall and Mr. Edward S. Reid for their assistance in and promotion of the endeavor. The author wishes to thank the former publisher of the *Brooklyn Heights Press,* Mr. Richard J. Margolis, for printing a series of the author's articles on Brooklyn Heights' period styles in the *Press* during the summer of 1959, which were expanded into Part I of this book. The writer also would like to acknowledge his indebtedness to the staff of the library of the Long Island Historical Society, where most of the research was done, with special recognition to the head librarian emeritus, Miss Edna Huntington, for stimulating discussions leading to considerably deeper insight into the phenomenon of old Brooklyn than could have been gained from any lesser source. Meriting much credit, too, are several authorities in their various fields, who were good enough to read the manuscript during its preparation and to impart valuable suggestions toward its improvement. This group includes Miss Maud Esther Dilliard, Mr. Meredith Langstaff, Mr. Alan Burnham, and Mr. Henry Hope Reed, Jr. The author also thanks Mr. Philip Formica for his help on checking the listings of houses, which are described as they existed on 1 January 1960.

Clay Lancaster
Brooklyn Heights
23 March 1960

Introduction

Brooklyn Heights: A high singular bluff, upward of fifty feet, extending from Doughty to Joralemon street, nearly half a mile in length, affording a commanding view of the city of New York, and where may be had a most delightful view of the bay, harbor studdied [sic] *with shipping, and the surrounding shores and distant hills of New Jersey.*
—*Samuel H. Cornwell,* The Brooklyn City Register, or Guide for 1848: Containing General Information. . . . *Brooklyn, 1848.*

BROOKLYN Heights presents a false front to the world. First of all, the name "Brooklyn" holds the popular connotation of a place where a certain tree grows and people talk with a funny accent. The word "heights" can mean almost anything, suggesting to the uninitiated an assumed snobbery compensating for the commonplaceness of the other term. From the harbor, East River, or Brooklyn Bridge, Brooklyn Heights appears composed of the thin horizontal planes of the Brooklyn-Queens Expressway and the Esplanade, and the bulky upright masses of hotels, apartment houses, office buildings, and a few industrial plants stationed around its perimeter. These impressions belie the charm of the real Brooklyn Heights, with its tree-shaded streets and bluestone-paved walks lined by rows of fine old brick and brownstone houses behind decorative iron fences, and distinguished churches in the romantic styles, dating back to an era when this was the most easily accessible, desirable, and aristocratic suburb of New York. One gets an entirely different concept of the community from within than from any of various vantage points outside its boundaries.

Brooklyn Heights is an irregularly shaped area situated on the

VIEW OF BROOKLYN HEIGHTS, WITH UNDERHILL'S COLONNA

1. Brooklyn Heights in 1853. Engraving showing Underhill's Colonnade Row and the burning of the Gowanus Building. Courtesy Long Island Historical Society.

promontory of Long Island directly across from the lower tip of Manhattan. At its greatest it is about eight blocks wide and fourteen long, its western extremity determined by the cliff overlooking the East River, its southern boundary by Atlantic Avenue, and its eastern and northern limits by Court and Fulton streets. The arc of Fulton Street cuts off the northeast corner of Brooklyn Heights as it turns toward the landing of the old ferry that plied between the Fulton streets of Manhattan and Brooklyn. The thoroughfare on this side was known as Ferry Road before acquiring the name of the inventor who mechanized the ferryboat.

The Fulton Street ferry was only one of three connecting Brooklyn Heights with Manhattan. The second and third ferries carried passengers from the base of Montague Street to Wall Street and from Atlantic Avenue to South Ferry. The Atlantic Avenue ferry was the terminal of the Brooklyn-Jamaica Railroad. From 1842 to 1859 the last mile of this line ran through an underground tunnel, thus becoming the world's first passenger subway. The railway was placed below ground to preserve the character of Atlantic Avenue, which in those days was a fashionable shopping street. The tunnel ended at a two-storied frame depot built in 1836 and demolished in 1914. Although unused for a century, all but the eastern extremity of the subterranean vault over the two-way tracks is said to remain intact (Long Island Historical Society Scrapbooks: II, p. 111; III, pp. 157–59).

Today, traffic between Long Island and New York flows through Battery Tunnel at the foot of Atlantic Avenue, and over Brooklyn Bridge above Fulton Street, and Manhattan Bridge a few blocks upstream, thus avoiding the Heights and leaving its predominantly residential streets to the relative quiet of local transportation.

Except for the variable outline in the northern part, and the peculiar angles of Joralemon Street, connecting the dock section with Borough Hall, and Love Lane, Brooklyn Heights is laid out on a rec-

2. Nos. 155, 157, 159 Willow Street. Photograph by Edmund V. Gillon, Jr.

tangular grid scheme. Blocks were planned 250 feet to the side, though less than a dozen, in the northwest section, turned out square. Omission of streets originally conceived resulted in the remaining blocks, some forty, having two to three times the prescribed length. The blocks between Clark and Pierrepont streets, and those between Joralemon and State, west of Clinton, have a north-south axis, whereas the balance have an east-west axis. Brooklyn Heights touches the civic center and S. Parkes Cadman Plaza on the east. Along most of the west side extends the Esplanade, which is cantilevered out over two levels of the Brooklyn-Queens Expressway and Furman Street. The Esplanade affords a magnificent view of South Ferry and the skyscrapers of Manhattan's financial district opposite, a vista up the East River to the north, and across the New York harbor to Governor's, Liberty, and Ellis islands, New Jersey, and Staten Island on the south.

The history of Brooklyn Heights as a residential suburb began soon after the establishment of a steam ferry plying between New York and Brooklyn in 1814. At that time a number of landowners, whose memories are perpetuated through such street names as Middagh, Pierrepont, Hicks, Remsen, and Joralemon, began dividing their respective holdings into 25×100-foot building lots. The first village map, recorded by Jeremiah Lott in 1816, the year Brooklyn was incorporated as a village, shows virtually the same street arrangement that exists today north of Clark Street, except for the crook to Orange Street at the Fulton Street end; and the Poppleton and Lott map of the Pierrepont estate, made three years later, indicates in a general way the present layout of the southern section of the Heights. This area, however, was still not much developed when a new map of the Pierrepont estate was made in 1831 by Isaac T. Ludlam, the village surveyor. All streets on the Heights were given their definitive form by about mid century, and they have remained unaltered down to the time of the construction of the Brooklyn-Queens Expressway during the early 1950's, which took off the northwest and southwest corners of the Heights.

Not a single building existing on Brooklyn Heights today figured on the Lott map of 1816 or the Lott and Poppleton map of 1819, barring perhaps part of No. 39 Henry Street not visible from outside. A good many structures stood on Fulton Street in those days, and

3. View of Heights from Brooklyn Bridge. Note steam elevated train and tower of Fulton Ferry Building in right foreground. From Art Work of Brooklyn, New York, *Chicago, 1896.*

several farm houses and villas were inside the range of the Heights proper, but all have since disappeared. However, a number of buildings put up soon after the Lott surveys were made are still to be found. The first scene of consecutive building operations was along the northern end of Hicks Street and on the cross streets adjacent to it. A large percentage of the early houses were of frame construction, such as Nos. 38, 40, 68, 70, and 72 Hicks Street and Nos. 24, 27, 29, 55, 57, and 59 Middagh Street. Contemporary brick examples include No. 51 Hicks Street and Nos. 43, 45, 55, 57, 82, 155, 157, and 159 Willow Street. The last three were built relatively far away from the center of activities, and were ironically aligned to a lane that no longer continues through to Willow Street, which makes them slightly askew with the street they face. In the paving under the gate of the middle house of this trio, No. 157, are set little squares of glass forming the skylight to the tunnel that connected No. 159 with its pre Civil War carriage house three doors away (No. 151). These row houses, with their small patches of greenery in front, seem to express the type of dwelling that was intended for Brooklyn Heights at the time of its development as a suburb more readily accessible to commercial New York, centered below City Hall, than most of Manhattan prior to the advent of railways many years later.

Although the row house predominated, there were some early builders who did not wish to restrict their dwellings to the narrow-plot pattern, and therefore constructed homes of a type requiring open space on all four sides. No. 13 Pineapple Street is one of the oldest, and later examples include Nos. 70 Willow Street and 36 Pierrepont Street, and the former Leavitt-Bowen mansion, with its massive Corinthian portico facing the harbor, that stood near the north side of Clark Street between Columbia Heights and Willow Street. Brooklyn Heights became famous for having some of the most substantial residences in Greater New York, and remained primarily a neighborhood made up of private houses, handsome churches, several elegant hostelries, such as the former Mansion House and Pierrepont House (sites of the present Mansion House apartments and Hotel Bossert), and a few corner groceries and taverns, until almost the close of the nineteenth century, when clubs, banks, large apartment buildings, and business houses invaded the area. In spite of the intrusion Brooklyn Heights still retains much of the pleasant atmosphere of opulent bygone days, which will be preserved only so long as its century-old houses are able to maintain some measure of their original character.

PART ONE

The Passing Parade of Period Styles in Brooklyn Heights Architecture

4. No. 135 Joralemon Street. Photograph by Edmund V. Gillon, Jr.

EXISTING buildings on Brooklyn Heights built during the forty-year period from 1820 to the eve of the Civil War exemplify the various architectural styles then in vogue in America. Houses dating from the first decade and a half of that period invariably followed the persisting colonial tradition and are referred to as "Federal" in style. Beginning about 1834 the Greek Revival mode put in its appearance here. The Greek Revival embodied a bolder and more architectonic treatment than the Federal, and was inspired by the antiquities of the Hellenic civilization rather than by those of the Romans. During the 1840's romanticism was manifested through the use of the Gothic and Romanesque revivals, derived from medieval European building. The Romanesque manner was introduced into America on Brooklyn Heights in a distinguished example that still stands, but the style did not amount to very much, here or elsewhere, until the last quarter of the nineteenth century. The Gothic Revival, on the other hand, flourished alongside the Greek, and remained vital long after the taste for classicism had shifted from the Greek to the Renaissance Revival, that had developed out of the simpler Italianate style around the middle of the 1800's.

In the next few pages will be given a more detailed analysis of these various centenarian styles, and also a glimpse into the later modes that have left their mark upon the older buildings through remodeling. Examples cited in parentheses are representative and not exhaustive of the characteristics considered. A list of the periods involved, together with the approximate dates of their span of existence on the Heights, is as follows:

5. No. 24 Middagh Street. Note carriage house at right.

A. Styles Employed in Buildings Upwards of a Hundred Years Old
- FEDERAL (1820–35)
- GREEK REVIVAL (1834–60)
- GOTHIC REVIVAL (1844–65)
- ROMANESQUE REVIVAL (1844–1900)
- ITALIANATE (1849–1860)
- RENAISSANCE REVIVAL (1850–1900)

B. Later Styles
- RUSKINIAN OR VENETIAN-GOTHIC (1867–69)
- "QUEEN ANNE" (1880–1900)
- COLONIAL REVIVAL (1890–1940)
- NEO-CLASSIC (1892–1940)
- MODERN PERIOD (1890–)

The Federal Style (1820–35)

FEDERAL is the term applied to the style used in architecture throughout the United States following the American Revolution and establishment of our federal system of government. It bridges the gap between the architectural mode of the Colonial period and the Revival styles (especially the Greek Revival) that came into full force during the second quarter of the nineteenth century. One phase of the Federal style is very formal, featuring tall columns and impressive porticoes, and is rightfully referred to as Classic Revival. One sees it in the work of Charles Bulfinch (State House in Boston), Thomas Jefferson (Capitol in Richmond and the University of Virginia colonnades at Charlottesville), Dr. William Thornton (Capitol in Washington), James Hoban (White House), and others.

In the existing Federal architecture of Brooklyn Heights, as in Manhattan, the classic elements are played down, though columns, or rather small slender colonnettes, may be seen sustaining mantel shelves and flanking front doors to residences (No. 24 Middagh, Nos. 126, 155, 157, 159 Willow, and No. 94 Remsen). These have been combined with other traditional elements, such as rustication, paneling, carved sunbursts, floral motifs, dentils, and various moldings, including cornices and entablatures, sometimes made break-front.

The Federal period provided the standard plan of the row house utilized on Brooklyn Heights (as elsewhere in American cities) until well into the twentieth century. The normal twenty-five-foot breadth of building lots here could accommodate the size of one room and a hallway wide enough for a staircase to one side. The result was the three-bayed house, having the front door off center, which was usually two rooms deep (No. 24 Middagh, Nos. 55, 57, 155, 157, 159 Willow, No. 135 Joralemon). In this species of dwelling the kitchen was usually located below stairs. With two full stories above the basement, a garret also was provided for extra sleeping quarters, either for children or servants. The roof ridge ran parallel with the street (in the English manner), and light and air for these top apartments were admitted through dormer windows piercing the front and back slopes of the roof, which ofttimes was double pitched (in the Dutch manner) for added space (No. 24 Middagh, No. 68 Hicks, Nos. 144, 157 Willow, and No. 135 Joralemon). Houses were built either of wood, frame covered with clapboards (the three single examples last cited), or of brick (the two on Willow), in either case on stone or brick foundations and with brick chimneys rising above the roofs.

Arched windows (dormers to Nos. 50, 51 Hicks) and fan doorways (Nos. 13, 17 Cranberry) appeared during the Federal period, the lunettes, or semicircular, or semielliptical transoms invariably leaded originally in attractive patterns (No. 126 Willow). Entrance stairs were either of wood or stone (brick was never used for treads), and of course only the stone examples have survived without replacement. Steps had a rounded molding at the top of the riser called a nosing.

6. Entrance detail of former house on site of No. 135 Willow Street (photographed in 1952).

Railings were fashioned of wrought iron, decorated with small cast-iron fittings, such as rosettes, and pine-cone or pineapple finials atop posts. Entrance stairs followed four distinct forms, which, for convenience, are referred to in the house analyses comprising the main body of this study as "Type A," "Type B," etc., following the table listed here:

A. stoop in front of doorway with stairs to one side (No. 84 Willow)

B. stairs on axis perpendicular to door, the lowest step having voluted ends, over which the railings make a horizontal spiral to a newel post (no example from the Federal period remains on the Heights)

C. also frontal, there are cage posts set on or at the ends of the lowest step serving as newels for the railings which join them; these open-work cage posts often combine rococo-gothic tracery in their side panels with pagoda tops (Nos. 155, 157, 159 Willow)

D. again frontal, the first step is flanked by stone pedestals surmounted by iron basket urns; the railings are not connected with these forms (house formerly on site of No. 135 Willow, No. 13 Cranberry—urns missing)

A house of the early period that is like a country dwelling is the shingled example at No. 13 Pineapple Street, having a central transverse stairhall with rooms to either side. Perhaps moved here from an earlier site, the house has been given several additions. The top row of larger windows in the rear indicates that the third floor was added around the middle of the nineteenth century. The front cornice and doorway date from the end of the century, and the low fanlight over the door is modern.

Wooden houses can be altered so easily by any hammer-and-saw carpenter that it is the exception rather than the rule to find an old frame house in anything like its pristine condition. The Heights is fortunate in having No. 24 Middagh Street and No. 135 Joralemon Street with so few changes, though the first-floor front windows of the latter have been enlarged to go with the Civil War era cast-iron porch. The Joralemon Street house still retains its early back porch, which is flanked by a pair of tiny projecting closets, probably the oldest structure of this kind on Brooklyn Heights.

The Greek Revival Style (1834–60)

THE GREEK Revival style made its debut in America in the Bank of Pennsylvania, an Ionic temple-front edifice designed by the English emigrant architect, Benjamin Henry Latrobe, and built in Philadelphia in 1799. As its name implies, inspiration for the new manner came principally from the ancient architecture of the Greeks, though Roman and Egyptian elements were incorporated to minor degrees as well. The principal source of authoritative designs for contemporary architects was the publication of James Stuart and Nicholas Revett, four volumes of plates, entitled, *The Antiquities of Athens,* issued in London from 1766 to 1816, with a supplement in 1830. The Greek Revival style was heavier and more masculine than the Federal, in part due to technical advances, whereby steam-powered machinery took over much of the work formerly executed by hand. The architect, therefore, became the designer of details as well as the planner of the building as a whole, and this consolidation of the two separate functions of builder and decorator into a single individual made for greater design unity. Architects belonging to the Greek Revival movement include Latrobe's two pupils, William Strickland (Merchants' Exchange, Philadelphia) and Robert Mills (Washington Monument), and the New York firm of Ithiel Town and Alexander J. Davis (U. S. Customs House, now Federal Hall Museum, Wall Street) among numerous others.

The Greek manner, never very popular in England or continental Europe, was warmly received in America, in part due to its associa-

7. Brooklyn City Hall (now Borough Hall).

tion with the free city states of Greece as opposed to the imperialism proper to Rome. It became virtually the national architectural style throughout the settled portions of the United States during the mid decades of the nineteenth century. It effected the disuse of graceful arches in domestic building; and attenuated colonnettes and fine carving around doorways and fireplaces were replaced by wide, flat moldings, slightly battered out at the bottom, with "Greek ears" at the top, or thick-set, plain pilasters supporting entablatures abbreviated sometimes to the point of crudity. The colossal-order portico was the earmark of Greek houses in the country or on large city lots, and was often featured on public buildings of the period, and sometimes on row houses as well.

The Greek Revival came to Brooklyn Heights about the time of the purchase of the site for the new city hall in 1834. Containing about three-quarters of an acre of land, the triangular lot bounded by Joralemon, Fulton, and Court streets at first was intended to receive a building strongly reminiscent of the New York City Hall (in the classic style of Louis XVI) built by Mangin and McComb in 1805, though the Brooklyn version was to be smaller and less distinguished looking. Foundations were commenced, but the project was abandoned. Other plans were submitted, such as a transitional Corinthian design by John Johnston and Edward Jones, whose drawings, dated 1 February 1842, are in the collection of the Long Island Historical Society. Three years later a gentleman styling himself "R. Butt, architect and lithographer," issued a booklet proposing an unusual scheme, a hollow triangular edifice encircling the whole block, having shops on the ground floor and the city offices above, a portico centered on each façade, and turret accents atop each of the rounded corners. But the design that was finally realized was by Gamaliel King, a Brooklynite who had been listed as a grocer up through the 1830 city directory, and afterwards listed as a carpenter. The building conceived by King bore a slight resemblance to the earliest plan, being rectangular and composed of several pavilions on a high basement; but its architecture was pure Greek Revival, rather than the Louis XVI style of the New York City Hall. A giant, shallow Greek Ionic portico dominated the north front. Set on a steep flight of steps, its six columns rose through three stories, and supported a full entablature crowned by a low-pitched pediment. Wings of the building extended out five bays on either side, and a circular cupola accentuated the central axis. The original cupola (presumably of wood) was replaced by one of iron about 1898. Except for this one element the present building exhibits little change today from its appearance when completed in 1848.

The style of the new city hall supplanted the Federal in the evolution of the row house. For the most part it made use of a higher basement, which henceforth included the family dining room on the same floor with the kitchen, leaving the two rooms of the main level to serve as twin parlors. There was a new sense of interior spaciousness. Ceilings were made higher, and a screen of columns or pilasters flanking wide sliding doors between the parlors allowed them to be thrown together into a single large apartment. The recessed front entrance was introduced, forming an intervening volume between outer and inner space. Houses were usually increased to three full stories above the basement, the third-floor windows sometimes worked into the frieze of the entablature (No. 56 Middagh, Nos. 51, 53 Cranberry, and originally No. 70 Willow). Parapet walls between chimneys masked the lower-pitched roofs of corner houses (No. 20 Willow). Row houses often had superimposed open galleries along their back side, each unit separated by a brick wall, which also screened the last one on the block from the adjoining street. Embodying most of these traits is the row of four houses inclusive of Nos. 20–26 Willow Street.

Of course in some ways the Greek Revival merely carried on the classic tradition set by the Federal style. This shows up nowhere bet-

8. Nos. 22, 24, 26 Willow Street.

9. Rear view of No. 20 Willow Street group from Middagh Street.

ter than in the entrance stairs, where steps retained the same type of nosings; railings became more elaborate but utilized many of the identical ornaments. Four of the seven forms of stairways that figured during the Greek Revival period were similar to the four varieties noted in the Federal era, and are therefore correspondingly designated "Type A" through "Type D." The last three are new additions to the list:

A. stoop in front of entrance with stairs to one side, the steps descending in a curve (No. 15 Willow and No. 18 Cranberry)
B. frontal stairs, the lowest step having voluted ends, with railing making a horizontal spiral to a newel post (Nos. 174, 176 Hicks)
C. also frontal, with cage posts at the ends of the first step (No. 260 Henry, if original)
D. frontal, with pedestals flanking first step surmounted by basket urns (No. 46 Monroe Place, No. 51 Cranberry, and No. 109 State—urns missing from last two)
E. also frontal steps, end blocks flank the first three or four steps on which the railing ends in a vertical volute (Nos. 42, 44, 46, 69, 71 Willow)
F. also frontal, blocks flanking lower steps have rounded front ends over which the railings make a horizontal volute (Nos. 39–52, 61–67 Joralemon)
G. again frontal, volutes of railing turn over truncated columns (No. 121 State)

Type E stairs, which are prevalent throughout the Heights, are practically unique to this area, indicating them to have been the design of a local concern. As a matter of fact they were advertised in the 1841 Brooklyn city directory as the product of the G. W. Stilwell Foundry, located on Fulton Street facing Front Street.

The professional architect came into his own during the Greek Re-

10. Entrance to No. 18 Cranberry Street. Note foot scraper near newel post.

11. Entrance detail of No. 42 Willow Street. Typical example of "Type E."

vival period, and the best known name closely associated with Brooklyn Heights is that of Minard Lafever, whose acknowledged works in this neighborhood, however, are in the Gothic Revival style, including Packer Collegiate Institute (1854), Church of the Holy Trinity (1844–47), and the two churches on Monroe Place. Whatever his style preference was for institutional and religious buildings, it is clear that he advocated the Greek Revival for domestic architecture, as shown in two of his publications, *The Modern Builder's Guide* (1833), and *The Beauties of Modern Architecture* (1835), the latter perhaps exerting a greater influence upon American architecture of the mid nineteenth century than any other single volume. Undoubtedly Lafever designed and built houses on Brooklyn Heights. The residence at No. 27 Pierrepont Street, despite recent remodeling, still has an exquisite frieze over the doorway of the front parlor reflecting a design given in both Lafever books, making use of an anthemion motif derived from the north doorway of the Erectheum on the Acropolis. Another smaller detail, equally attributable to Lafever, adorns the side entrance to the house on the west corner of Sidney Place at State Street (No. 107). Several Heights residences, such as No. 92 State Street and 98 Joralemon Street, have a circular plaster centerpiece in the front-parlor ceiling modeled after Plate 21 in *The Beauties of Modern Architecture*.

Greek Revival is the predominant style among buildings on Brooklyn Heights and is usually manifested in adjacent houses, like the No. 20 Willow Street group. An unusal exception meriting attention is No. 70 Willow Street, a three-storied brick building four bays wide, which throws the pilastered doorway off center, having a side yard on the south flank, the site of a later stair tower. The plan of No. 70 Willow Street is that of a country villa, featuring a circular staircase in a lateral extension to the hall. Across the back of the house is a porch having slender Federal-type columns, which is difficult to account for

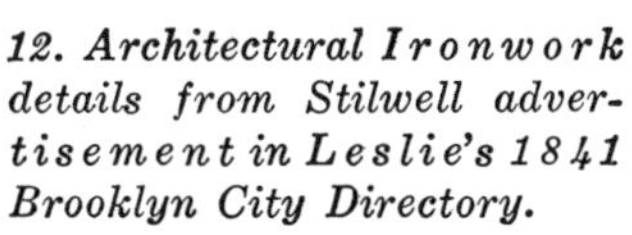

12. Architectural Ironwork details from Stilwell advertisement in Leslie's 1841 Brooklyn City Directory.

13. Ceiling centerpiece design. From Minard Lafever, The Beauties of Modern Architecture, *New York, 1835.*

14. Nos. 79–85 Remsen Street.

inasmuch as the house was completed in 1838, and everything else about it belongs to the Greek Revival or later periods. Similar plans are to be found in the houses at No. 90 State Street, No. 56 Livingston Street, in the duplex Nos. 108, 114 Pierrepont Street, and once were in several others, now altered.

We are indebted to the Greek Revival period for many of the attractive iron fences along the streets on Brooklyn Heights. Thin square bars are fashioned into frameworks in which rectangular spaces are filled with frets, meanders, guilloches, and floral forms in double relief, with pointed uprights resembling obelisks, or a cresting on top made up of cones or anthemions (No. 97 Clark, No. 101 Willow, No. 71 Pierrepont, Nos. 11 and 51 Cranberry, No. 92 State, and No. 261 Henry).

The Gothic Revival Style (1844–65)

THE GOTHIC Revival came to America simultaneously with the Greek, and was fostered by the same architect, Benjamin Henry Latrobe, in a country villa, called Sedgeley, built in what is now Fairmount Park, Philadelphia, in 1799. The Christian style—as the gothic is sometimes referred to—is thought of mostly in connection with churches, which makes all the more remarkable its introductory use here in a residence. Employed previously in England, it was encouraged there through the appropriation of sizeable sums of money under the British Church Building Acts passed by Parliament during the early nineteenth century. The Gothic Revival also was the romantic style par excellence, which awarded it a firm place in the fabrication of picturesque houses, as in Sir Walter Scott's Abbotsford (1812). Scott's Waverly novels and the verses of the "graveyard poets" did much to popularize the style in every quarter of the English-speaking world.

15. Minard Lafever's Church of the Saviour, Pierrepont Street at Monroe Place. Lithograph by E. Bisbee. Courtesy First Unitarian Church.

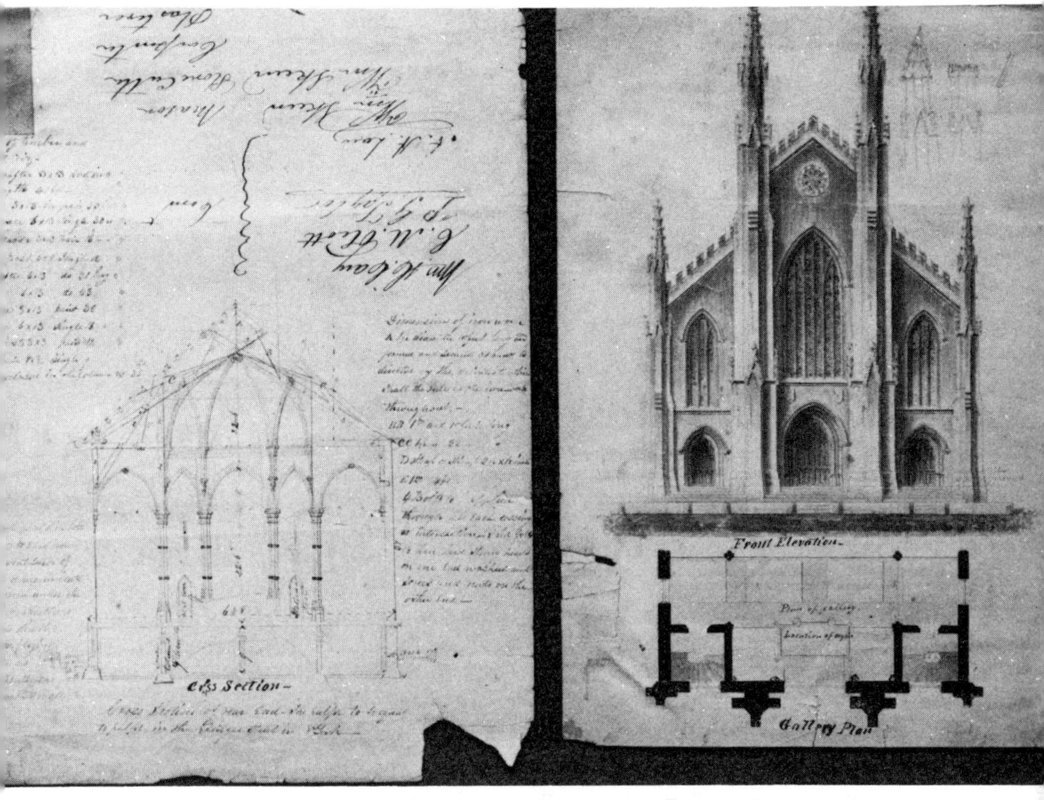

16. Page of specifications and architect's elevation drawing for Church of the Saviour. Courtesy First Unitarian Church.

The foremost American advocate of the Gothic Revival for domestic architecture was Andrew Jackson Downing, who resided near Newburgh, New York, where he wrote voluminous tomes about country living and horticulture, most influential of which, as regards building, was his book, *The Architecture of Country Houses* (1850).

The Gothic Revival got its start on the Heights in two churches begun in 1844 by Minard Lafever, Church of the Holy Trinity and Church of the Saviour. Within a half-dozen years the style was being adopted for the row house, Tudor arches with carved spandrels replacing pilastered doorways, slender clustered colonnettes flanking the sliding doors between parlors, and medieval window tracery offering models for plaster ceiling centerpieces and iron railings (Nos. 118, 120, 122 Willow). It is interesting to compare the cast-iron railings and fences of the mid nineteenth century with the rococo-gothic wrought-iron work of earlier date (cage posts, No. 155 Willow), the spidery, two-dimensional treatment of interlaced arches having given way to architectonic ribs and sculpturesque crockets, plastically treated forms made possible through the casting technique.

Externally the least modified Gothic Revival house on Brooklyn Heights is the three-storied brownstone residence at No. 131 Hicks Street, which has a twin adjoining it, No. 135. Their doorways are recessed beneath low pointed arches, with horizontal hood molds of the Perpendicular period surmounting them, and appearing also over the windows. The windows of No. 131 retain their center mullions. The newel posts, however, are missing their finials, which probably were similar to the spires on the posts to the entrance steps of No. 167 Clinton Street. The three brick houses on State Street just west of Sidney Place are also well preserved, though stripped of their hood molds over the openings. Only No. 107 of this group still boasts its first-floor balcony railing, but all three display a quantity of iron-tracery stair rails and fences.

The first four houses on the west side of Willow Place, beginning at the corner of Joralemon Street, apply the Gothic Revival style in a rather unusual way. These small, three-storied brick buildings have coupled entrance porches with clustered colonnettes supporting Tudor arches with spandrels pierced by trefoils. The ironwork railing remaining on the porch nearest Joralemon Street encircles a newel post in a manner proper to classic designs, but the details are medieval, consistent with other parts of the entrance shelter. Second- and third-floor windows are contained within shallow vertical recesses, and are known as "Daviséan windows" after the originator of the motif, Alexander Jackson Davis of New York, one of the architects of the Customs House on Wall Street, mentioned earlier, and of numerous villas in the romantic styles along the Hudson River and elsewhere. He was also the designer of many of the house plans published in the

Downing books. The plain walls, rectangular voids, and simple cornices of the Willow Place houses are without stylistic affiliations, so that the gothic elements could be easily removed and we would have a structure hardly suspected of ever having been gothicized.

Another application of Gothic Revival design distinguishes the house at No. 36 Pierrepont Street, a cubic brick mass set back from the sidewalks. Tracery panels and hood molds cap the windows, and traceried railings embellish the second-floor rear gallery and brownstone front porch. The steps of this porch have been removed to allow for a ground-floor entrance, and a section of the former stair rail has been inserted in the space between the front corner posts, which accounts for the axis of the main quatrefoil in it leaning at a rakish angle. An admirable shallow-roofed balcony of delicate ironwork is attached to the Hicks Street side of the house, and a long stretch of appropriately patterned fencing encloses the yard along both streets.

No. 52 Livingston Street, across from the rear of Packer Collegiate Institute, is a simple brick dwelling that was later made quaint with gothic details, much as Washington Irving employed a pseudo Dutch style in remodeling Sunnyside. The front parlor was converted into an octagon, with niches in the corners; and the room is entered through a recessed doorway in the narrow hall, which protrudes into the parlor in such a way as to balance the chimney breast opposite. The polished black marble mantel with end buttresses has a Tudor arch over the fireplace opening. Ribs radiating from the centerpiece on the flat ceiling give the impression of a low vault or dome. The second story of the façade is crowned with a lancet-arched water-table or cornice, above which rises a modern attic. Hood molds punctuate the windows, and the dipping roof of the shallow porch spanning the first story is upheld by lacy gothic ironwork, the railing of which harmonizes with the matching fence that borders the sidewalk a few feet in front. The versatility of the Gothic Revival can be understood by

17. Balcony on side of No. 36 Pierrepont Street. Photograph by Edmund V. Gillon, Jr.

18. Nos. 131, 135 Hicks Street. Among the Heights' finest residences in the Gothic Revival style.

glancing in turn at this tiny residence, and then at the large Packer building opposite, the construction of which, in 1854, may have prompted the stylistic changes to the small house. Metal casement windows and stucco on the front wall constitute relatively recent "improvements."

The Gothic style, unlike the Greek, survived the trying Civil War period. During the late 1860's it took on special characteristics and passed into a new phase, which will be discussed later as the Ruskinian or Venetian Gothic.

The Romanesque Revival Style (1844–1900)

THE ROMANESQUE Revival never enjoyed as much popularity in the United States as did the Gothic Revival, its heaviness limiting its suitability mostly to large public buildings. The majority of its examples date from the last quarter of the nineteenth century, due to the influence of the work of Henry Hobson Richardson of Boston, designer of the famous Trinity Church (1872) of that city. Often the Revival is referred to not as Romanesque alone, but as Richardsonian Romanesque. A ponderous treatment of masonry walls pierced by few round-headed openings enframed by wide bands of low-relief carvings or moldings distinguish the Romanesque from the buttressed, lighter-walled Gothic Revival with its many pointed arches.

Brooklyn Heights has a special claim to the Romanesque Revival since it possesses what is considered to be the first building constructed in this style in America, the Church of the Pilgrims (now Our Lady of Lebanon) at Henry and Remsen streets. The Church of the Pilgrims was conceived in 1844 by Richard Upjohn, who later designed Grace Church and the mansions on Pierrepont Place, in the Gothic Revival and Renaissance modes respectively. The clean-cut, gray stone forms of the Romanesque essay, relieved by cornices and simple details

19. *No. 82 Pierrepont Street, Herman Behr's house, now enlarged into Hotel Palm. From* Architecture and Building, *2 May 1891.*

I pass this every morning on my way to work!

around the entrances, make the Church of the Pilgrims one of the outstanding landmarks of Brooklyn Heights. Unfortunately, the tall steeple once capping the corner tower has been removed, and the windows have been changed.

The Romanesque manner made little impression upon the domestic architecture of Brooklyn Heights before the Civil War, a rare exception being the cornice of Nos. 119, 121 Henry Street, but it became the vehicle for several noteworthy examples built toward the close of the century. One of these is the Herman Behr house on the southwest corner of Pierrepont and Henry streets, a composition of stone, brick, terracotta, and tile created in 1890 by the architect Frank Freeman, who also designed the Hotel Margaret (1889), at Columbia Heights and Orange Street, and the Jay Street Fire House (1891), beyond Borough Hall, in the same idiom. The Behr house has been enlarged into the Hotel Palm. Another good example of a residence on the Heights that is Romanesque is No. 6 Pierrepont Street, having a monumental entrance staircase with stylized plant reliefs superbly carved upon its rounded stone posts, and with bold wrought-ironwork railings on the parapets between these forms.

The century-old house on the Heights most affected by the Romanesque Revival is the east half of the duplex facing Monroe Place, No. 114 Pierrepont Street. The front wall of this unit, which was originally Greek Revival, was entirely rebuilt around 1887, leaving only the floor levels to testify to the kinship that existed between it and its neighbor.

The Romanesque Revival is best adaptable to civic buildings, and Brooklyn's distinguished example is the original south section of the main post office on Washington Street, built by M. S. Bell in 1891, to which a large wing was added by James Wetmore in 1933.

The Italianate Style (1849–1860)

NOT ALL mid-nineteenth-century American buildings were given as much stylistic embellishment as those of Greek, Gothic, and Romanesque revival persuasions. The nineteenth century was not one to act freely on matters pertaining to taste, and the authority for simplicity, like the Revivals themselves, had to be substantiated by an existing tradition. It was found in what might be termed secondary buildings of Italy, buildings that had a background every bit as venerable as the ancient temples, plus the advantage of a living present. Reference is made to the informal dwellings of the sub-nobility classes, that dot the Italian landscape and that have maintained certain basic characteristics since the Etruscan and early Roman periods. They feature plain walls, usually stuccoed, pierced by clean-cut windows and protected by low-pitched roofs with deep overhanging eaves supported on brackets. Often the composition was asymmetrical, which fitted in nicely with the picturesque setting. The first appearance of this style in the United States was a design published, by coincidence, in the earliest American work to present the Greek orders, John Haviland's *The Builder's Assistant,* issued in Philadelphia from 1818 to 1821. The design in question is Plate 60 in the second volume of the three-volume set. It is a line drawing by the architect-author for the façade of a two-storied residence with a recessed entrance in a gabled central pavilion, and with a tiny one-storied wing appended to each flank, unadorned except for the use of small columns at the entrance, and beam ends or brackets, supporting the thin cornices. Such a house was built eight miles out of Philadelphia for John Cridland.

In New York State this simplicity of styling was taken over by one Orson Squire Fowler, a resident of Fishkill, who conceived a compact and economical species of dwelling in the shape of an octagon, as presented in his book, *A Home for All; or, the Gravel Wall and Octa-*

gon Mode of Building, 1848. This book, which came out in six later editions during the next ten years, caused the insertion of eight-sided house plans in a number of contemporary books by other authors, and influenced the erection of prismatic domiciles throughout America.

The plain Italianate style came to Brooklyn Heights in Plymouth Church on Orange Street, built by the architect J. C. Wells in 1849. It is a barn-like, two-storied structure of red brick, having a raking cornice with brackets in front, and a wide segmented blind arch spanning the three center entrance bays. The church contained the largest auditorium in Brooklyn, and was used for secular as well as for religious meetings. Here Henry Ward Beecher preached. The portico existing today is later. It is interesting to note that Plymouth Church exerted an influence in its immediate neighborhood. On the south side of Orange Street, one block westward, was erected a row of five houses (Nos. 22–30) during 1850–51 which are as austere and devoid of Revival details as Plymouth Church itself. Even the cast-ironwork fence and stair railings have been reduced to the simplest lines.

The Renaissance Revival Style (1850–1900)

THE CLASSICISM of the Federal period had been a sort of final ebbing of the Renaissance, that had started in Italy at the end of the thirteenth century, and was transmitted to North America through England during the late seventeenth and eighteenth centuries. Although this phase of classicism was eclipsed by the Greek Revival during the second quarter of the 1800's, toward the middle of the century it was to be resurrected as a competitive Revival style. Moreover, it remained active throughout the balance of the nineteenth century, long after the Greek had passed into oblivion. The Renaissance Revival, as it is called, also has a close connection with the

Italianate style, just described, the archetypes for both coming from the same country.

The Renaissance Revival is distinguished from the other styles of Mediterranean inspiration by a certain opulence, manifesting itself in an increased scale—often limited mainly to extreme ceiling heights by lot restrictions—and an abundance of ornamentation, especially around openings. Some of these features, such as capitals, friezes, and consoles, are embellished with lush carvings of acanthus leaves and less orthodox forms of vegetation (Nos. 218, 220 Columbia Heights and Nos. 114, 138, and 140 Remsen). Balustrades replaced other kinds of railings. The half-round arch was reintroduced at entrances, though spanning recessed vestibules instead of flush doors as in the Federal period (compare No. 220 Columbia with No. 126 Willow). The segmented arch was used occasionally over both doors and windows (No. 104 Pierrepont). A popular Renaissance Revival building material was brownstone, which, being porous, does not weather well, and in time requires renovating with stucco. Anticipating this, a contemporary substitute for architectural details and balustrades was the more durable cast iron, which, when given successive coats of paint and sand, could hardly be distinguished from stonework (iron balustrades at No. 220 Columbia Heights, No. 17 Cranberry, Nos. 35, 37 Remsen, and No. 134 Joralemon). The streets having been paved during the late 1840's, footscrapers, such as were incorporated into earlier railings, were omitted from balustrades.

The Renaissance Revival began to appear on the Heights soon after the Gothic Revival was adapted to residential buildings here, and the architect responsible for the finest domestic examples was none other than one of the two important builders of medieval-type churches, Richard Upjohn, designer of the Church of the Pilgrims (Romanesque Revival, 1844) and Grace P. E. Church (Gothic Revival, 1847), the

20. No. 220 Columbia Heights (in foreground).

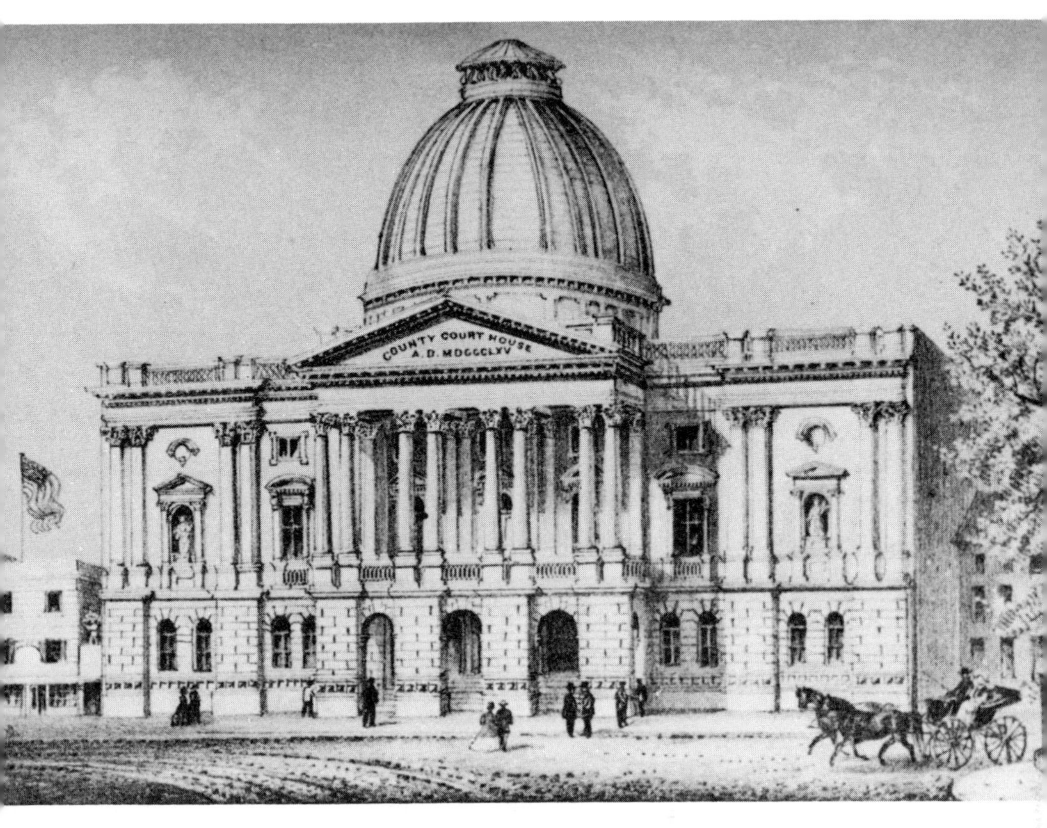

21. King's County Court House. The date in actual pediment reads "A. D. MDCCCLXI." From Report of the Building Committee...of the County Court House, *Brooklyn, 1866.*

latter on Hicks Street at Grace Court. To Upjohn are attributed three great houses erected on the river side of Pierrepont Place, two of which are still standing, the Henry E. Pierrepont mansion, which was on the site of the playground, having been razed in 1946. The pair of remaining houses (also attributed to Frederick A. Peterson) have a brownstone facade of ample proportions, crowned by a deep entablature, having quoins at the corners. The windows are enframed in moldings surmounted by a projecting cornice on a section of plain frieze. The wide front doorways are given importance through the use of coupled Corinthian pilasters set on engaged pedestals to either side, and broad flights of steps with balustrades leading up from the street. In spite of the symmetry of their façade, the plans of the two houses are different. The north side of the northern house is a flat plane, whereas the south side of its mate is an articulated, irregular composition of brick and stone and ironwork, with a projecting pavilion at the far end and a long, low arcuated conservatory. The rear of this building, for years the home of the Low family, is one bay wider than its counterpart.

A composition formed by three houses in the Renaissance Revival style is at the northwest corner of Pierrepont (Nos. 21, 23, 25) and Willow streets. The five-storied brownstones, each two bays wide, are tied together by a continuous balcony, once balustraded, across the first-floor level, above the rusticated ground story, and by an elaborate console cornice with a pediment crowning the centermost house. These buildings have been spoiled by later bay windows and a fire escape. A number of single houses around the corner on Columbia Heights and along Remsen Street, as well as the stately row on the east side of Montague Terrace (after 1870) are in the same mode.

A public building in the Renaissance Revival style is the County Court House behind City Hall. It was built in 1861 after a plan by the architect of its neighbor, Gamaliel King, and a collaborator, Herman Teckritz. The Court House has a high rusticated basement story and is entered through constricted arches in the base of the great portico, which features coupled Corinthian columns unifying the second and third stories and supporting an entablature and pediment above. A balustrade surmounts the entablature, and an ovoid dome crowns the central axis. The difference in treatment between the classic of the Renaissance Revival and the Greek Revival is well demonstrated through a comparison of the Court House with City Hall. The City Hall design taken from the Greek temple lays stress upon the regularity of a modular unit, through evenly spaced columns in the portico, and the same spacing carried over into the fenestration. The Court House composition based upon a Renaissance villa or palace introduces variety into its arrangement of solids and voids with columns and pilasters set in pairs and diversified window treatment. The principle of diversity is more difficult to apply to the set pattern of the row house, but it was achieved through details, such as different hoods over the windows for every story (Nos. 114, 138, 140 Remsen).

A French rather than Italian Renaissance element much used in residences on the Heights is the mansard roof, a steeply pitched roof that disguises a full top story. Its name derives from the seventeenth-century architect, Jules Hardouin Mansard, who created the section of the Palais de Versailles containing the famous Galerie des Glaces. There had been an unsuccessful attempt to build a baroque-manner residence with a mansard roof in Philadelphia at the close of the eighteenth century, the so-called Marble Palace of Robert Morris, designed by the French architect, Pierre Charles L'Enfant, who later was to plan the City of Washington, D.C. Perhaps the oldest existing mansard roof in the United States is that added to the Cabildo in New Orleans during the mid 1840's. It is doubtful whether one put in an appearance on Brooklyn Heights much before a decade later. Probably one of the earliest is that on the brownstone house at No. 113 Remsen Street, built about 1854, followed soon afterwards by a more impressive version on the large brick-and-stone house four doors away (No. 123), which is now the home of the Brooklyn Bar Association. Most Heights mansard roofs belong to the post Civil War era.

Ruskinian or Venetian-Gothic Style (1867–69)

AMONG the later-nineteenth-century styles, the one that rightly may be termed a phase of a more important and enduring Revival is that touched off by the English critic, John Ruskin, through publication of his two essays on architecture, *The Seven Lamps of Architecture* and

Stones of Venice, which came out in America almost as soon as in England, about 1850. Ruskin was a literary figure and not an architect, and stated his appeal wordily on moral and aesthetic grounds. His was the typical Victorian viewpoint that "architecture" was decoration applied to structure, which came to mean that "good" architecture preferred an abundance of it. It was Ruskin's love of Venice that captivated the imagination of Western Europeans and Americans, and led to a switch from seeking prototypes in the medieval monuments of England (and France) to the more highly colored pre Renaissance buildings of Italy. The Ruskinian style has the pointed windows of the Gothic Revival proper, but is distinguished by the alternating blocks of white and brown voussoirs in these arches, and by the horizontally banded stonework in two colors. The effect looks somewhat Oriental, yet should not be confused with the Saracenic style. Brooklyn Heights' two principal examples of the Venetian type of gothic are the Brooklyn Mercantile Library (currently a branch of the Brooklyn Public Library) on Montague Street, by Peter B. Wight, and Saint Anne's P. E. Church adjoining Packer Collegiate Institute on the corner of Clinton and Livingston streets, by Renwick and Sands. Both buildings were begun in 1867 and completed two years later. The library is about to be demolished at the time of this writing. The Ruskinian style had very little effect upon domestic architecture.

The "Queen Anne" Style (1880–1900)

IN COMPARISON to the Revivals, each of which followed a clearly defined precedent, the "Queen Anne" was a strange mixture, capable of adopting elements from almost anywhere. This was partly due to the fact that it had no strong champions, like Latrobe for the Greek, Downing for the domestic Gothic, or Ruskin for the Venetian. It was also due to the lack of specific models, such as the ancient temples of Greece and Rome, or the medieval monuments of England. Its name was taken from the British queen who ruled at the beginning of the eighteenth century, but many features of the late-nineteenth-century style to which it was attached came from buildings of the Stuart period of the seventeenth century, when gothic effects were combined with Renaissance details. The hybrid Sparrowe's House at Ipswich, England, comes as close as any to having the main features that were borrowed, including medieval-type pargeting and gabled roofing, and a flat bay window, subdivided into a small-scale Palladian motif, with rounded ends (No. 62 Montague and Nos. 168, 170 State).

The best manifestation of "Queen Anne" on Brooklyn Heights is the group of three houses inclusive of Nos. 108–12 Willow Street, the end house bearing the date 1883 in a panel on its south flank. Treated as a single irregular mass of brick, stone, terracotta, and shingles, interest is achieved through a full orchestration of bay windows, towers, gables, chimneys, and a variety of openings, rectangular, arched, and elliptical. Unlike the Revivals the accent in "Queen Anne" is not upon style for its own sake, but upon unusual harmonies of forms, colors, and textures, in which respect it foreshadowed the viewpoint of the early twentieth century, and became itself a style developed from a no-particular-concern for styles.

A personal touch that crops up during the "Queen Anne" period is a type of decor associated with the English architect, Sir Charles Eastlake (1836–1906). Used in both furniture and buildings the characteristic member is a long, flat molding, usually having a reeded central section, enframing panels in doors and elsewhere. There is also a pierced foliage design, like jigsaw work in thin wood, as often as not carved into stone lintels or overdoor friezes (No. 56 Pierrepont, No. 123 Remsen).

22. No. 109 Willow Street.

The Colonial Revival Style (1890-1940)

THE COLONIAL Revival in America, like the "Queen Anne," drew upon an architecture of a bygone day, though one that was not of any remarkably great age, going back only a few intervening generations. However, the Colonial Revival differed from all the other imitative styles in that its source of authority was indigenous. The factor of nationalism enters the picture, perhaps accounting for the occasional sentimentality over individual features that prompted the misuse and poor scaling of details. The Colonial Revival had its real beginning in the "celebrated" tour made by the architectural firm of McKim, Mead, Bigelow, and White to examine the Georgian houses of New England in 1877.

A characteristic example of the Colonial Revival on Brooklyn Heights is the four-storied house at No. 109 Willow Street, built by John Petit about 1905. The front wall is an admirable piece of Flemish-bond brickwork with dark headers. Stone lintels have been borrowed practically verbatim from the Federal houses farther down the block (Nos. 155, 157, and 159), but a comparison between the old and new buildings reveals that the details of the latter are sadly out of scale with the façade. The columns in the doorway are oversized, whereas the squeezing of the transom into the frieze of the entablature goes to the other extreme. The size of the main cornice, which seems taken from the late-nineteenth-century bracketed crowning on the frame dwelling next door, looks better on the brick house, which is a story taller; but the relief moldings under the modillions are so delicate that they are practically lost from the street. On the whole the elevation of No. 109 Willow Street is a self-conscious design.

The Colonial Revival shows up most often on Brooklyn Heights in fan doorways added to mid- or late-nineteenth-century houses (No. 143 Willow, No. 37 Remsen, No. 10 Garden Place), sometimes recessed behind rectangular openings (Nos. 13, 15 Monroe Place). The Parish House of Plymouth Church, built in 1913 at the corner of Hicks and Orange streets, is a commendable specimen of a Colonial Revival public building.

The Neo-Classic Style (1892–1940)

THE GRANDEUR of the "White City," which was the popular name for the group of exhibition halls at the World's Columbian Exposition at Chicago in 1892–93, gave rise throughout America to a renewed vogue for classic architecture, that had survived only in modified form, combined with other elements (as in the Renaissance Revival). What characterized the resurgence was its insistence upon purity, and a bigness of scale made possible through the erection of great arches, vaults, and domes describing spacious interiors. The architecture of the Chicago Fair was unified by a standard-sized colossal order sixty-feet tall. The adoption of the classic style for the buildings of the exposition was largely due to the persuasion of East Coast architects, such as Daniel Burnham, Richard Morris Hunt, and McKim, Mead, and White.

The first and foremost example of this neo-classic on Brooklyn Heights is the Brooklyn Savings Bank, built on the northeast corner of Pierrepont and Clinton streets in 1893–94 by Frank Freeman, architect of the Hotel Margaret and Mr. Behr's house of a few years earlier, both in the Romanesque idiom. The Brooklyn Savings Bank follows closely the precedent set at the Chicago Fair, having been begun, actually, while the exhibition was still in progress. It has a mausoleum-like magnificence, its entrance a triumphal arch, not unlike the portal to Hunt's Administration Building at the Columbian Exposition. The great banking room is covered by an oblong dome surmounted by a columned gallery clerestory, the space below flowing out into attached vaults on four sides.

The second building on the Heights showing the influence of the White City is the former People's Trust Company, now the First National Bank, at Nos. 181, 183 Montague Street, planned and built by Mowbray and Uffinger in 1904–5. It displays a temple façade, its engaged tetrastyle portico having Roman Ionic columns set on pedestals, and its pediment filled with sculptured figures. An attic story rises above the pediment.

The third Heights building indebted to the new classicism adjoins the second one on Montague Street and runs the whole length of the block along Clinton Street to Pierrepont, its north entrance facing the Brooklyn Savings Bank. Originally the home of the Brooklyn Trust Company, and now the Manufacturer's Trust, the building externally resembles an Italian Renaissance palazzo with rusticated walls, massive arched windows, and a columned attic. It has exquisitely tooled gray marble and beautifully detailed ironwork at its two portals. The strictly neo-classic feature in this building is the vast barrel-vaulted hall that fills most of the volume and is richly ornamented, with a coffered ceiling and an unusually fine cosmatesque floor. Built in 1915 by Edward Palmer York and Philip Sawyer, its interior may have been inspired by the vaulted hall in the Pennsylvania Railroad Station (1906), New York, founded upon the Tepidarium of the ancient Baths of Caracalla, and the exterior suggested by the New York State Building at the Chicago Fair, modeled after the Villa Medici in Rome, in which case both sources of inspiration would have been buildings by McKim, Mead, and White.

The Modern Period (1890-)

THE BUILDERS of modern times have done more to mar than to enhance the appearance of Brooklyn Heights. A few residences built around the turn of the century add some interest to the architectural melee here, such as the house on the northeast corner of Clinton and Schermerhorn streets, reminiscent of severe city dwellings designed by the contemporary Chicago school, and No. 129 Joralemon Street, built before 1893 by Harvey Murdock for David Chauncey. This stone and yellow-brick residence combines picturesque massing of the Romanesque Revival with delicate Colonial Revival details, and has a bungalow feeling in addition.

Most modern work, however, has been destructive, either pulling down the fine old houses to replace them with bare-faced apartment buildings, or, almost as bad, lowering their entrances, stripping off their architectural details, and covering their fronts with stucco.

Also, on the edge of Brooklyn Heights, adjacent to Borough Hall, there have sprung up variously treated tall office buildings of questionable scale, which group got off to a good (or bad) start upon construction of the nine-storied Romanesque Revival Franklin Trust Company Building at Montague and Clinton streets in 1891. It includes such other oddities as the modern gothic Insurance Building at No. 130 Clinton Street (undoubtedly responding to the style of Packer Collegiate Institute and Saint Anne's Church, across from it), and the Chase Manhattan Bank at No. 185 Montague Street, embellished with a geometric type of ornamentation featured at the French Arts Décoratifs Fair of 1925, held at Paris four years before its construction.

PART TWO

The Streets of Brooklyn Heights and Their Century-Old Houses

North-South Streets

COLUMBIA HEIGHTS

PIERREPONT PLACE

COLUMBIA PLACE

WILLOW STREET

WILLOW PLACE

HICKS STREET

GARDEN PLACE

HENRY STREET

MONROE PLACE

SIDNEY PLACE

CLINTON STREET

West-East Streets

MIDDAGH STREET

CRANBERRY STREET

ORANGE STREET

PINEAPPLE STREET

CLARK STREET

PIERREPONT STREET

MONTAGUE STREET

REMSEN STREET

GRACE COURT

JORALEMON STREET

LIVINGSTON STREET

SCHERMERHORN STREET

STATE STREET

Columbia Heights

(Supplementary illustrations nos. 48–54)

COLUMBIA Heights takes its name from the former Hezekiah Beers Pierrepont estate, facing the harbor, that lay approximately between what is now Remsen Street and Love Lane. The original Columbia Street, indicated on the Trustees Map of the City of Brooklyn (1819), extended in a straight line along the crest of the cliff from Fulton Street to Joralemon Street, with building lots on each side. The present Columbia Heights runs southward from Everitt Street (the first block below Fulton Street at its northern extremity) to Pierrepont Street, where it makes a slight bend, and continues to Montague Street as Pierrepont Place, and from Montague to Remsen as Montague Terrace. A continuation between Joralemon and State streets is called Columbia Place.

The earliest houses were built near the Fulton Street end. The oldest existing ones are three row houses on the east side above and three on the west side below the intersection of Pineapple Street (Nos. 111, 113, 115, and 140, 142, 144), predating 1840. Also before 1840 was built Underhill's elegant group called Colonnade Row, on the east side between Middagh and Cranberry streets. Across Cranberry Street stood one of America's first Turkish-bath establishments. The David Leavitt mansion, constructed in 1844 and better known for its later owner Henry C. Bowen, with its colossal Greek Corinthian portico toward Columbia Heights, occupied the south half of the block bounded by Pineapple, Clark, and Willow streets. Colonnade Row burned in 1853, the Turkish bath closed in 1913, and the Leavitt-Bowen mansion was razed in 1904.

Brick, brownstone, or frame residences of the mid nineteenth century on the west side of Columbia Heights had back yards that extended out onto the tops of warehouses fronting Furman Street below; other warehouses stood across Furman Street, and beyond were wharves in the East River for the ships that sailed to foreign ports. The warehouses on the west side of Furman Street were torn down in 1958, following the fate of those across the way a decade earlier. Today, an industrial plant, near the north end, several dormitories, and modern apartment houses detract from the good appearance of Columbia Heights. The outstanding building of the post Civil War period here is the Hotel Margaret on the northeast corner of Orange Street, designed by the architect Frank Freeman, and built in 1889 of stone, brick, terracotta, and copper in the Romanesque Revival style. The building lost much of its colorfulness when its polychromy was covered by a neutral-toned coat of paint during remodeling in 1958.

west side

138. 3-storied brownstone, Rence. Revival details, console cornice, segmented arched windows, frieze and cornice over enframements, curved pediment on consoles over doorway; house indicated on 1860 map (No. 96) but number could not be found listed in city directories up to 1863; ironwork modern.

140, 142, 144. 3-storied row houses with continuous brick façade, Greek Revival, brownstone Corinthian pilasters and entablatures enframing recessed doorways, steps Type E; listed in 1840 city directory house guide (n[ear] Pineapple) respectively as homes of James Freeland (No. 98 in 1845 directory), Peter Hoffman and Henry Sheldon, all indicated to have been merchants; late XIX cent. mansard roofs, door alterations, plate-glass windows; doorway of No. 144 badly weathered.

162, 164. 3-storied row houses, continuous brick façade, Greek Revival, corniced labels over windows, door enframement with "Greek ears," stairs Type F; No. 164 listed in 1844 city directory (n[ear] Clark) W. G. Sterling, merchant (No. 120 in 1845 directory); No. 162 in 1846 directory (No. 118) Benjamin B. Blydenbury, merchant, and John H. Brower; No. 162 has contemporary fence, later

23. The Leavitt-Bowen mansion from Columbia Heights. Razed in 1904. Courtesy Long Island Historical Society.

mansard roof, No. 164 has 4th story added, entrance lowered; both have plate-glass windows.

166. 3-storied brick, high basement; listed in 1844 city directory (No. 122) Henry E. Pierrepont (previously had lived at mother's house on Pierrepont Street opposite Willow); 4th story added, entrance lowered, plate glass.

170. 3-storied brownstone; house on site listed in 1844 city directory (No. 124) Horace B. Claflin; present building probably post Civil War, Rence. Revival window frames capped by frieze and cornice, pediment on brackets over recessed entrance, mansard roof.

176, 178. 3-storied frame row houses, shingled; Italianate style, cornice hood molds over windows, pair of square piers supporting small entrance porches, stairs Type B, iron railings; No. 178 listed in 1845 city directory (No. 128) George L. Sampson; No. 176 listed in 1846 directory (No. 126) Thomas B. Merrick, home of Henry Ward Beecher 1851–55; modern box vestibule replaces porch on No. 178, also new ironwork, brick retaining wall in front; No. 176 given modern brick veneer, "Regency" entrance porch and details (1938); retains original cast-iron railings.

192. 4-storied brownstone, Rence. Revival details, console cornice, segmented arched windows, frieze and cornice over window enframements, arched pediment on consoles over doorway (altered); rear cast-iron

24. Architectural ironwork designs. Note "Roman veranda" in center. Advertisement from Smith's Brooklyn City Directory *for 1855.*

porch (visible from Esplanade) identical with "Roman Veranda" design in Phenix Iron Works advertisement, 1855 city directory; listed in 1856 city directory (No. 134) Michael Cusack, mason, and Charles Gorman, painter; ironwork modern.

194. 3-storied brownstone, Rence. Revival details, console cornice, segmented arched windows, frieze and cornice over window enframements, arched pediment on consoles over doorway, balustrade; listed in 1862 city directory (No. 138) C[amden] C. Dike.

196. 4-storied; listed in 1853 city directory (No. 140) Jonas Gunderson, stevedore; details obliterated, stuccoed, entrance lowered.

198. 3-storied; listed in 1856 city directory (No. 142) Henry J. Cutbill, furrier, Andrew McCormick, clerk, and Thomas R. O'Connell, packer; details obliterated, wall stuccoed, 4th floor added, entrance lowered.

200. 3-storied brick; listed in 1846 city directory (No. 144) Bushrod Birch (had been listed No. 146 in 1845 directory, n[ear] Pierrepont in 1844 directory); this or a nearby house indicated in 1840 directory (n[ear] Pierrepont) Mrs. Eliza Hawkins; 4th story added, entrance lowered, casement windows 1st story.

202. 3-storied; listed in 1846 city directory (No. 146) Samuel Ingle [see No. 200 Columbia Heights]; 4th story added, pediment on brackets over entrance, plate glass in windows, casements 1st story, ironwork modern.

210. 3-storied brownstone, Rence. Revival details, console cornice, segmented arched windows, frieze and cornice above enframements; listed in 1852 city directory (No. 150) Andrew Graff, shoemaker (perhaps indicated in 1840 directory, n[ear] Pierpont [*sic*], Mrs. Rosanna Adams); doorway composed of Corinthian columns supporting entablature and arched pediment, rustication etc., late XIX cent.; ironwork modern.

212, 214. 3-storied brownstones, Rence. Revival details, rusticated basement, arched windows with frieze and cornice, arched pediment on consoles over doorway; listed in 1860 city directory (No. 152) Coe Adams, provisions, and John Bullard, broker, and (No. 154) Arthur W. Benson; No. 214 has story added, entrance lowered.

220. 3-storied brownstone with mansard roof and tower, Rence. Revival details, arched windows with frieze and cornice over enframements, arched pediment on consoles over entrance, iron balustrades; house indicated on 1860 map (No. 160) but house number could not be found in city directories up through 1862; modern French doors.

east side

111, 113. 3-storied row houses, continuous brick façade, Greek Revival, pilastered recessed doorways, entrance steps Type E; presumably listed in 1837 city directory as "c[orner] Pineapple," Samuel Wood, bookseller (in 1840 directory, n[ear] Pineapple, Samuel S. Wood, bookseller, also G. S .Wood, merchant); No. 113 has 4th story added, both have late XIX cent. bracketed cornices, arched doors, plate-glass windows; hood cornices above windows stripped.

115. 4-storied brick, similar to adjoining house; originally had posts at base of entrance steps; listed in 1844 city directory (No. 93) William W. Seymour; later bracketed cornice, bay window on south flank, doors and plate glass, modern iron railing and fence.

145, 147. 3-storied, continuous brick façade; Greek Revival, Corinthian columns supporting entablature enframing recessed doorway, stairs Type E (?), corniced labels over windows, contemporary fences; No. 147 listed in 1842 city directory (n[ear] Clark) Charles and Cyrus Bill (No. 119 in 1845 directory); No. 145 in 1844 directory (No. 117) John Haviland; No. 145 has later door, iron balustrade railing; No. 147 4th floor added, entrance lowered; both plate-glass windows.

149, 151. 3-storied, continuous brick façade, high basement; similar to No. 153 group; No. 149 listed in 1846 city directory (No. 121) W. F. Jones; No. 151 in 1847 directory (No. 123) Benjamin M. Sherman, merchant; No. 151 has been altered, entrance lowered.

153, 155, 157. 3-storied, continuous brick façade, high basement; Greek Revival, pilastered doorways, stairs Type E, corniced labels over windows, contemporary fences; Nos. 153, 155 listed in 1844 city directory (No. 125) James W. and John Elwell, merchant, and (No. 127 n[ear] Clark) Warren and George Hastings, merchant; No. 157 in 1845 directory (No. 129) Elizabeth Radcliffe, widow; Nos. 153, 157 later doors; No. 153 has entrance lowered; all plate glass.

161. 4-storied brick; listed in 1844 city directory (No. 131) Daniel Ayres, merchant; bracketed cornice, entrance lowered, pediments on brackets over windows.

173. 3-storied; listed in 1849 city directory (No. 141) Warren Carpenter, merchant; 4th floor added, wall stuccoed, entrance lowered, plate glass in windows.

175. 3-storied; listed in 1849 city directory (No. 143) Albert Woodruff, merchant; 4th story added, entrance lowered, wall stuccoed, plate glass in windows.

Pierrepont Place

(Supplementary illustration no. 55)

PIERREPONT Place was conceived as a continuation of Columbia Street across the H.B. Pierrepont estate, though the second block was not opened until 1870 and called Montague Terrace. Three great Renaissance Revival residences were built on the west side of Pierrepont Place, the work of architect Richard Upjohn or Frederick A. Peterson. One of the three, the Henry E. Pierrepont mansion, was demolished in 1946. The east side of the street is occupied by modern yellow-brick apartment buildings.

west side

2, 3. 4-storied duplex of ample proportions on high basement, continuous brownstone façade, Rence. Revival details, including deep entablature, quoins, windows enframed and surmounted by frieze and cornice hoods, coupled Corinthian pilasters flanking entrances, balustrades to entrance stairs; No. 3 has arcuated conservatory, projecting wing of brick and stone south flank, one bay wider across rear than its mate; built 1856–57 by Richard Upjohn, arch.; listed in 1858 city directory, No. 2 residence of Alexander M. White, furs, and No. 3 residence of A[biel] A[bbott] Low, teas; Alfred T. White listed as living at No. 2 from 1868 to 1880, when he moved to his own house, No. 40 Remsen Street.

Columbia Place

ONE BLOCK long, connecting the present west end of State Street with Joralemon, Columbia Place is dominated by the six-storied Riverside Houses running two-thirds the length of the west side of the street. A low-rent housing project built for Alfred T. White by William Field & Son, architects, in 1889–90, the Riverside Houses accommodated 19 stores and 280 two- to four-room apartments. The west unit was demolished for the construction of the Brooklyn-Queens Expressway. On the east side of Columbia Place is an assortment of low brick and frame houses, including four of the nine units of Cottage Row (Nos. 7–13) built during the late 1840's. A few brick flats near the south end date from a little before the Civil War, but are not included in the following list because of the confusion in numbering that existed here on Columbia Place at that time, making it impossible to determine references to specific occupants of these buildings in contemporary city directories.

east side

7, 9, 11, 13. Small 3-storied clapboarded frame row houses with shallow porches, each 2 bays wide, triple windows alternating with front doors in 1st story; survivors of 9 similar structures originally referred to as "Cottage Row"; 1848 city directory lists No. 7 (2 Cottage Row) Ezekiel Morrell, painter, No. 11 (6 Cottage Row) John Hughes, milkman, and No. 13 (8 Cottage Row) G. Lomer, fur merchant; No. 9 listed in 1849 directory (4 Cottage Row) Walter Dixon, pilot, South Ferry; Nos. 7, 9, 13 covered with asphalt shingles, No. 11 stuccoed.

Willow Street

(Supplementary illustrations nos. 56–58)

THE HICKS brothers originally planned Willow Street to extend only between Middagh and Clark streets. In 1818 the Brooklyn trustees wished to continue it to State Street, but Hezekiah B. Pierrepont wanted to maintain long blocks running in an east-west direction across his estate, and the scheme still prevails. Willow Street takes up on the south side of the former Pierrepont estate, the stretch from Joralemon to State Street going by the name of Willow Place.

Gabriel Furman wrote that there were eleven dwellings and four stables on Willow Street in 1821. One of the few houses still in existence on the Heights listed in the first city directory of 1822 is No. 84 Willow Street. Other houses almost as old are the Federal row dwellings at Nos. 43 and 45, 55 and 57, and 155, 157, and 159, all built of brick laid in Flemish bond. Of the same vintage is the curb-roofed

25. Nos. 2, 3 Pierrepont Place. Photograph by Edmund V. Gillon, Jr.

frame house on the southeast corner of Middagh Street, having a carriage house behind on Willow Street. The best surviving Federal fanlight doorway of Brooklyn Heights belongs to the house at No. 126, which has the additional features of an urn carved in relief on a stone plaque over the arch of the front door, and presumably early ironwork railings and cage posts capped with pine cones to either side of the entrance steps.

A fine row of Greek Revival city houses occupies the north end of the west block below Middagh Street. These buildings have open galleries or porches at the back, a characteristic once prevalent in this area. A contemporary device more nearly unique to Brooklyn Heights is the frontispiece composed of stone steps with pedestal-like blocks flanking the lower treads and a wrought-iron railing embellished with cast-iron rosettes terminating in a vertical swirl over the end projections. Specimens are to be found at Nos. 42, 44, 46, 69, 71, and 101 Willow Street. A Greek Revival house on the northeast corner of Middagh displays a stoop at the entrance reached by a stairway curving to one side. An even better example is the one at the southwest corner of Cranberry. No. 70 Willow Street is a large Greek Revival house four bays wide, with a plan like that of a country house, with a circular staircase placed laterally in the hall, similar in arrangement to No. 90 State Street and several others on the Heights.

Nos. 118, 120, and 122 Willow Street are brownstone houses styled in the Gothic Revival mode of the 1850's. The tracery ironwork of their front fences should be compared to the more delicate rococo-gothic of the cage posts of No. 155, which are at least two decades earlier. There are a number of oversized buildings along Willow Street, but, except for the harsh pile at the southwest corner of Orange Street, the slightly less objectionable pile at No. 135, and the remodeled doorway of No. 149, these do not detract too much from the atmosphere of the street. Some even may be said to add interest to it, especially the turrets of the Towers Hotel, which are illuminated at night like a maharaja's palace.

west side

20, 22, 24, 26. 3-storied row houses, continuous brick façade; Greek Revival, door enframements with "Greek ears" surmounted by low-pitched pediments, recessed entrances, 4-panel doors flanked by plain pilasters, side lights and transoms; stairs modified Type D perhaps once

26. No. 57 Willow Street.

having additional ironwork on projecting antapodia (urns?); tall windows main floor 6 over 9-paned sashes; parapet wall connects chimneys of end house on Middagh Street; screen wall to 2-storied rear open galleries, garden wall common-bond brickwork; contemporary iron fences (cement curb on Middagh Street added May 1959); listed in 1847 city directory: No. 20 (No. 16) Howard C. Cady, lawyer (n[ear] Cranberry in 1846 directory?); No. 22 (No. 18) J. Bliss Rumrill, jeweler (n[ear] Cranberry in 1846 directory?); No. 24 (No. 20) Alfred G. Peckham (No. 32 Willow in 1846 directory); and No. 26 (No. 22) H. C. Hathaway, widow; No. 22 was home of Henry Ward Beecher in 1848.

28, 30. 4-storied brownstone row houses, each 2 bays wide, continuous façade, rusticated basement treatment to 1st story, console cornice, arched openings; No. 28 listed in 1858 city directory (No. 24) Benjamin F. Tilt, bookkeeper; No. 30 in 1859 directory (No. 26) Rebecca Wason, widow.

42. 3-storied, brick façade continuous with east flank of No. 18 Cranberry Street; Greek Revival; similar doorway, entrance steps Type E, contemporary fence; listed in 1845 city directory (No. 36) Thomas P. Bucklin; sashes to windows main floor changed, glass pane inserted in front door, pediment missing over doorway, bracketed cornice.

44, 46. 3-storied row houses having continuous brick façade; similar to No. 42; "Greek ears" to door enframement, railings simpler, fence has different fret in lower part; both listed in 1841 city directory (n[ear] Cranberry) Zachariah Lewis (Mrs. Z. Lewis, No. 38 in 1842 directory), and Alfred Edwards (No. 40 in 1843 directory); doors and cornices late XIX cent., plate glass in windows.

50. 4-storied on high basement, bracketed cornice; listed in 1853 city directory (No. 42) William M. Andrews, ice merchant; stuccoed, concrete railing and fence.

56. 3-storied brick on high basement, Greek Revival, pilastered doorway, steps Type B, iron fence same pattern as No. 42; listed in 1845 city directory (No. 48) Rev. William B. Lewis, pastor of the Third Presbyterian Church; front doors later.

70. 3-storied, 4 bays wide, brick Greek Revival with brownstone pilastered doorway and truncated column pedestals flanking entrance steps; listed in 1839 city directory (No. 58) Adrien Van Sinderen (previously lived corner Columbia Heights and Orange Street); 3rd-story front windows originally in frieze only, now enlarged; small-paned windows restored *ca.* 1953; stair tower on south side added about 20 years earlier; fan door and iron railings and fence late XIX cent.; porch across main floor rear has Federal-type posts; circular staircase (newel post late) and 4-

27. Doorway to No. 126 Willow Street.

room plan similar to No. 90 State, No. 56 Livingston; owned at present by Oliver Smith, noted theatrical designer.

80. 3-storied brick, high basement, stairs Type A; listed in 1849 city directory (Pineapple c[orner] Willow) George Chapman (No. 66 Willow in 1856 directory); bracketed cornice, bay over entrance on Pineapple Street, bay window 1st story Willow Street side, plate glass.

82, 84. 2-storied Flemish-bond brick on high stone basement, probably oldest existing duplex on Heights; No. 84 listed in 1822 city directory (n[ear] Pineapple) Christopher Codwise (No. 70 in 1825 directory); No. 82 in 1826 directory (No. 68) Silas S. Webb, shipmaster; steps, but not railings, of No. 84 perhaps contemporary, Georgian doorway not original here; plan on 1855 map shows rear porch between flanking closets similar to that remaining on No. 135 Joralemon Street; stairs of No. 82, like other remodeling, late XIX cent.; story added and window pattern of both changed, bracketed cornice.

104. 3-storied frame on high basement of Flemish-bond brickwork; listed in 1829 city directory (No. 88) Robert Spear (or Spier, 1834 directory), baker; heavy late XIX cent. bracketed cornice; modern renovations include small-paned windows, shutters, fan doorway, and iron railings.

118, 120, 122. 3-storied row houses having brownstone façade and Gothic Revival details, gorge cornice with bead-and-reel molding at base, drip molds over square-headed windows and recessed doorways, cast-iron tracery railings and fences; house on site of No. 120 listed in 1829 city directory (No. 102) David Leavitt, merchant; house on site of No. 122 in 1832 directory (No. 104) Joseph Sands; house on site of No. 118 in 1835 directory (No. 100) Peter W. Radcliffe; present form dates from *ca.* 1850; doors altered, windows plate glass, newel posts at base of entrance steps missing.

124. 3-storied Flemish-bond brickwork above stone foundations, originally probably similar to No. 126; listed in 1831 city directory (No. 106) Jeremiah Brown, Jr.; late XIX cent. Romanesque stone posts flanking entrance steps, ironwork modern; remodeled corbie-stepped gable comparable to No. 43 Willow Street.

126. 3-storied brick on stone foundations, Federal style, stone lintels over windows and stonework encasing arched entrance with double-leaf doors flanked by Ionic colonnettes and carved archivolt concentric to fanlight divided by molded leading; drapery swag carved on stone panel in wall above keystone of arch; vestibule several steps below level of main floor; wrought-iron fence and railings to Type C steps, rococo-gothic cage posts capped by pine cones may be old though fence replaces former balustrade; only surviving fan doorway of Federal period on Heights; listed in 1832 city directory (No. 108) C. W. Rockwell; lintels and basement stonework renovated, glass panels and modern handles on front doors.

136, 138, 140, 142. 3-storied row houses, continuous brick façade, high stone basement, corniced labels over openings, otherwise plain recessed doorways, stairs Type B, contemporary fences; 1840 city directory lists No. 138 (No. 120) William James, writing master, and No. 140 (No. 122) Infant School; No. 136 listed in 1843 directory (No. 118) Francis L. Hawkes, D. D.; No. 142 in 1844 directory (No. 124) George B. Elkins; No. 140 has 4th floor added, entrance lowered, fire escape on front, brick fence; Nos. 136, 142 have modern Colonial Revival doorways, plate glass in windows.

144. 4-storied, high basement; listed in 1851 city directory (No. 126) E. C. Boyd, school; modern yellow-brick facing, entrance lowered, brick fence.

148. 4-storied, high basement; listed in 1855 city directory (No. 130) George C. Mann, stationer; modern brick facing, entrance lowered, modern ironwork.

150. 3-storied, high basement, console cornice; listed in 1855 city directory (No. 132) Moses K. Moodey, furrier; stuccoed, modern ironwork.

east side

11. 4-storied brick on high basement, projecting bay on front, bracketed cornice; listed in 1854 city directory, F. W. Sargent, merchant; entrance lowered.

15. 3½-storied brick with parapet masking gable end towards street; Greek Revival, pedimented doorway having "Greek ears" to enframement, Type A stoop with curved stairs to side, contemporary iron railings and newel posts; cast-iron fence missing frets in lower frames: listed in 1834 city directory (No. 41 Middagh) William Kumble, leather merchant; south flank continuous brickwork with front wall of No. 23 Middagh Street.

43, 45. 2-storied row houses, continuous Flemish-bond brick façade: No. 43 listed in 1824 city directory (near Cranberry) William Lee, shipmaster (No. 35 in 1825 directory); No. 45 in 1825 directory (No. 37) Alexander Gordon, merchant; No. 45 has single-pitched roof pierced by dormers, changes include recessed doors and plate-glass windows; No. 43 has a corbie-stepped superstructure in pseudo-Dutch style, late XIX cent. ironwork.

55, 57. 2½-storied row houses having continuous façade laid in Flemish-bond brickwork, continuing around south flank of No. 57; tooled stone lintels above openings front and side, original size of 1st-story windows indicated by blind windows in south wall; parapet between chimneys masks gable; note key motif in frieze on axes with voids front of No. 57, also treatment of dormers; No. 57 listed in 1825 city directory (No. 47) Robert White, merchant; No. 55 in 1832 directory (No. 45) J. D. Wright; late XIX cent. changes include 3rd story with bracketed cornice of No. 55, ironwork of No. 57, and entrances, stoops, and plate-glass windows of both; railing of No. 55 is modern.

67, 69. 3-storied row houses, continuous brick façade; Greek Revival, "Greek ears" to door enframement; entrance stairs Type E; No. 69 listed in 1836 city directory (No. 55) Misses M. & S. Coe, boarding house; No. 67 in 1838 directory (No. 53) Foster Nostrand, merchant; No. 67 has later ironwork, cornice showing Colonial Revival influence; No. 69 has mansard roof; both have late XIX cent. doors, plate glass in windows.

71. 3-storied Flemish-bond brickwork on high basement; entrance stairs Type E; railings larger size than No. 69; listed in 1831 city directory (No. 57) Nathaniel Howland; mansard roof added, plate glass in windows, later doorway spoiled, steps without nosings.

73. 3-storied brick; listed in 1831 city directory (No. 59) Abraham Suydam; later bracketed cornice, walls stuccoed, entrance lowered, plate glass in windows.

101. 3½-storied brick, Greek Revival, pilastered doorway, steps Type E, elaborate contemporary fence with cast-iron rosettes, obelisks, and cones along top; listed in 1838 city directory (c[orner] Clark) Sheldon Leavitt, merchant (No. 81 in 1839 directory); door late XIX cent., full 4th story modern; part of screen wall to former back porch may be seen at northeast corner of building.

103. 3-storied brick, Greek Revival, doorway with "Greek ears," scrolled top, steps Type B; listed in 1848 city directory (No. 83) William M. Richards, merchant; 4th floor added.

113. 3-storied frame house; presumably listed in 1829 city directory (No. 95) Thomas J. Rudyard (identified as No. 93 on 1855 map; adjoining house was No. 97); mid XIX cent. cast-iron entrance porch and bracketed cornice; façade covered composition shingles.

143. 3-storied brick, high basement; listed in 1844 city directory (No. 113) Gardner Burbank; walls painted, keystones over 1st-story windows, Colonial Revival fan doorway and modern railings.

155, 157, 159. 2½-storied row houses, continuous Flemish-bond brick façade over stone basement, arched dormer windows in curb roof; Federal style, articulated stone lintels above door and window openings, 8-panel doors flanked by Ionic colonnettes, leaded glass transoms and side lights; Type C steps, with wrought-iron rails, rococo-gothic cage posts; iron fences Greek Revival period; orientation of houses askew due to alignment to former extension of Love Lane adjacent to north wall of No. 155; this house listed in 1826 city directory (c[orner] Love Lane) (?) Hitchcock, merchant (initial "C" given in 1829 directory); other two listed in 1829 directory (No. 127) Daniel Pomroy, and (No. 129) George Brinkerhoff; all three houses indicated (without identification) on 1831 map by Isaac T. Ludlam, village surveyor; minor changes, esp. lower wall; 3rd story added to No. 159; leading missing doorway of No. 157; **the glass set in the pavement near the gate to No. 157 is a skylight to a vault entered from under the stoop.**

Willow Place

A CONTINUATION of Willow Street, running between Joralemon and State streets, Willow Place is lined mostly with mid-nineteenth-century residences, which recently had been rooming houses until reclaimed for private dwellings. Of special interest are the row of four Gothic Revival houses at the northwest end of the block, and the four Greek Revival houses having tall, heavy porticos at the southeast termination, with a single remaining sister house that was part of a similar group opposite. The strong community spirit among the inhabitants of the Willow Place area has resulted in its becoming known as "Willow Town."

west side

2, 4, 6, 8. 3-storied duplexes with continuous brick façade; Gothic Revival, coupled porches having clustered colonnettes, Tudor arches with open spandrels, contemporary cast-iron traceried railings that encircle newel posts capped with crocketed spires (remaining on No. 2 alone); diamond-paned transoms and side lights to front doors; vertical recessed "Daviséan" panels decorated with chevron moldings unify 2nd- and 3rd-story windows; No. 6 listed in 1847 city directory, Edward Walter; others listed in 1848 directory, No. 2, (?) Graham, No. 4, James M.

Staples, commission merchant, and No. 8, J. L. Allien, merchant; because of angle of Joralemon Street No. 2 is narrower at back.

10, 12, 14. 3-storied row houses, continuous brick façade, plain doorways, entrance stairs Type B; Nos. 12, 14 listed in 1846 city directory (both as n[ear] Joralemon), William H. Moore (No. 12 in 1847 directory), and C. Roumage (C. C. Roumage, No. 14 in 1847 directory); No. 10 in 1847 directory, Michael Caffee, merchant; 4th story added to No. 10, plate-glass windows, best preserved ironwork; newel posts missing to No. 14, finials missing No. 12; pane of glass in doors of Nos. 10, 14 later.

16, 18, 20, 22, 24. Narrow 3-storied brick row houses, each 2 bays wide; void pattern similar to No. 7 Columbia Place (frame) and No. 40 Joralemon Street (brick) groups; 1846 city directory lists No. 20 (n[ear] Joralemon) Richard Haviland (No. 20 in 1847 directory), and No. 24 (Willow Place) M. B. Marckwald (No. 24 in 1847 directory); No. 18 listed in 1847 directory, Richard Vaughan, grain measurer; other two in 1848 directory, No. 16, Joseph H. Limburger, watchmaker, and, No. 22, H. C. Hathaway, widow; No. 20 retains original front door and triple window 1st story, though in bad repair; No. 16 presents best appearance.

42, 46. Survivors of row of four houses matching No. 43 group opposite: No. 42 listed in 1849 city directory (No. 40) Bernhard Westerman, bookseller; No. 46 in 1851 directory (No. 44) Jacob Wyckoff, merchant; No. 46 in poor repair; No. 42 has modern front added.

east side

1. 4-storied brick house, narrow and plain, north wall continuous with façade of No. 56 Joralemon Street, contemporary ironwork at entrance; listed in 1849 city directory, Thomas Frere, crockery dealer.

9, 11. 3-storied row houses, continuous brick façade, high basement, bracketed cornice, plain recessed doorways, stairs Type B, contemporary fences; No. 9 listed in 1857 city directory (No. 3) Charles B. Coffin, music; No. 11 in 1858 directory (No. 5) C. F. Chace, drugs; windows of No. 11 changed, door Colonial Revival.

13, 15. 3-storied, continuous brick façade, high basement, each house 2 bays wide, bracketed cornice, wreath in relief over plain recessed doorways (No. 15 only), stairs Type B, contemporary fences; listed in 1856 city directory (No. 7) Thomas Baker, and (No. 9) Pereze S. Steele, dry goods.

28. Entrance porch to Nos. 2, 4 Willow Place.

29. Nos. 43, 45, 47, 49 Willow Place. Photograph by Edmund V. Gillon, Jr.

23, 25. 3-storied brick row houses, segmented arch spanning voids with hood molds, entrance stairs Type B, bracketed cornices; listed in 1854 city directory, No. 23 (No. 21) William Owen, glass blower, and No. 25 (No. 23) S. J. Townsend; plate glass in windows; No. 23 has concrete railings.

33, 35, 37. 3-storied row houses, continuous brick façade, plain recessed doorways, stairs Type B; No. 35 listed in 1846 city directory (n[ear] State) J. S. Milford, merchant (No. 33 in 1848 directory); No. 37 in 1847 directory (No. 35) John Cole, sailmaker; No. 33 in 1848 directory (No. 31) Clevland Forbes, steamboat captain; No. 33 has fire insurance plate on wall; Nos. 35, 37 plate glass in windows.

39, 41. 3-storied brick row houses, plain recessed doorways, stairs Type B; both listed in 1848 city directory (No. 37) Eliza Freeborn, widow, and Thomas Freeborn, and (No. 39) Henry Pettibone, wool broker; lower part of tall windows of main story of No. 39 filled in, plate glass in 3rd-story windows.

43, 45, 47, 49. 2-storied brick row houses having continuous colossal-order portico with square wooden posts supporting deep entablature, porch floor only a step above ground level; Greek Revival, doorways without enframements, recessed pilasters flanking doors bear plain architraves; 1846 city directory lists No. 43 (near State) Charles A. H. Brown (No. 41 in 1847 directory), and No. 45 (near State) John Bayard, merchant (No. 43 in 1847 directory); No. 47 in 1847 directory (No. 45) William Tester; and No. 49 in 1848 directory (No. 47) Moses O. Allen, accountant; this group is the last surviving colonnade row on Brooklyn Heights.

Hicks Street

(Supplementary illustrations nos. 59–64)

ONE OF the two longest streets on Brooklyn Heights, Hicks Street was named by the two brothers John and Jacob Middagh Hicks after their family. It is one of the first streets in the area to have been built upon, to which a number of frame houses towards the northern end bear testimony. Gabriel Furman, in 1821, noted thirty-one dwellings, two groceries, one school house and two stables on Hicks Street. The blocks above Cranberry Street have always been largely commercial, and, having become run down, recently have undergone a resurgence through the appearance of several small galleries and art shops. Buildings subsidiary to Plymouth Church occupy the east block between Cranberry and Orange streets; and the towering mass of the Saint George Hotel dominates the scene two blocks beyond. A number of Greek Revival and a few Gothic Revival houses are on Hicks Street between Clark and Pierrepont, with occasional apartment buildings, the largest of which is Mansion House, constructed during the 1930's on the

30. Wood engraving of the old Mansion House hotel, Hicks Street. Courtesy Long Island Historical Society.

site of a hotel of the same name. The former building originally had been built in 1822 for a private residence, then had become the home of the Brooklyn Collegiate Institute for Young Ladies for a quarter of a century before serving as a hostelry, that was remodeled and enlarged in 1875. A row of stables belonging to the hotel, contemporary with its remodeling, face College Place behind Mansion House.

The Hotel Bossert stands on the east side of Hicks Street between Montague and Remsen streets, covering a little more than the area of the old Pierrepont House inn. Grace P. E. Church, built by Richard

Upjohn in 1847, and the court and alley opposite, to which the church lends its name, compensate for the bulky size and monotonous rows of windows of the modern apartment house facing the back of the Bossert. The west side of the last block extending southward to State Street begins with a row of "Queen Anne" houses built by Mrs. Packer in 1887, is followed by a handsome little fire-engine house with Renaissance details (1903), a row of earlier carriage houses, and ends with a group of mid-nineteenth-century residences. The site of the former Philip Livingston house is on the east side of Hicks Street, about where the orthopedic hospital now stands. A number of Greek Revival houses are still to be seen in this block, including Nos. 281, 283, which are annexes to the hospital.

west side

38. 3-storied frame, clapboarded; listed in 1830 city directory (No. 32) Joseph Bennett, packer; story added, late XIX cent. bracketed cornice; shop 1st floor; now in disrepair.

40. 3-storied frame house; listed in 1831 city directory (No. 34) Michael Vanderhoef, cartman; shop now 1st floor; composition shingles on wall.

48. 2-storied frame house; listed in 1829 city directory (No. 42) Peter Prest, boarding house; now 4-storied, stuccoed; 1st floor formerly grocery, at present art gallery.

52. 4-storied brick; listed in 1856 city directory (No. 46) Diederick Sanneman, shipmaster; 4th-story windows heightened, modern iron fence.

56. 3-storied frame, evidently originally a boarding house; listed in 1829 city directory (No. 48) Henry Barton, laborer, Weyman Johnson, blacksmith, and Alexander Stephenson; now 4-storied; altered early 1950's, given composition shingle front, metal windows, depressed porte-cochère.

60. 2½-storied frame with curb roof, front dormers similar to No. 51 across street; listed in 1829 city directory (No. 50) Edward Drew; front wall stuccoed; originally had fan doorway (arch remains), entrance now lowered.

66. 3-storied, front wall Flemish-bond brickwork, carved stone lintels over windows, south flank frame;

listed in 1829 city directory (No. 56) Reuben Hough, sash manufacturer, and Cyrus P. Smith, attorney & counsellor-at-law (mayor of Brooklyn 1839); Edward E. Collins' "Star Hotel" 1854–; mansard roof added, asphalt shingles south wall, store 1st floor.

68. 2½-storied frame with curb roof, doorway has Ionic colonnettes similar to No. 24 Middagh Street; listed in 1822 city directory (No. 52, c[orner] Cranberry) Jacob Hubbs, grocery and tavern; in 1824 directory (No. 52 c[orner] Cranberry) Elijah Raynor (No. 54 in 1825 directory); in 1830 directory (No. 58) Mrs. Bruce; walls now covered with asphalt shingles.

70. 2½-storied frame house; listed in 1839 city directory (No. 60) John R. Stogy, cabinet maker; renovated 1959, front shingled, entrance lowered.

72. 3-storied frame house; listed in 1826 city directory (No. 58) Richard Everit (No. 62 in 1829 directory); later bracketed details, front covered with composition shingles.

74. 3-storied brick; listed in 1839 city directory (No. 64) William I. Schenck, grocer; entrance lowered.

100. 3-storied frame; listed in 1826 city directory (No. 82) Donald Malcolm (No. 86 in 1829 directory); renovated 1959.

104. 4-storied, Flemish-bond brickwork front and north flank, high basement, parapet wall masking roof; listed in 1840 city directory (No. 90) Jacob Talman, Dr. M. Windell; entrance lowered.

146. 3-storied frame; listed in 1826 city directory (No. 116) Erasmus Kurtz, mathematical instrument maker (Erasmus A. Kurtz, No. 124 in 1829 directory); late XIX cent. bracketed cornice, modern alterations include "colonial" doorway.

148. 3-storied frame house; listed in 1830 city directory (No. 126) Edward Gregory, merchant; story added, bracketed cornice, stuccoed.

152. 3-storied brick, Greek Revival, entrance stairs Type E; Federal leading in transom and side lights to 6-paneled door in plain doorway, frieze windows to 3rd story; listed in 1840 city directory (No. 130) Peter Briggs; shown as frame house on 1855–60 maps (?).

158. 4-storied brick; listed in 1855 city directory (No. 136) Aaron Fields, clerk; molded stucco lintels over windows, entrance lowered, iron fence modern.

160. 3-storied brick on high basement; Greek Revival, "Greek ears" to front door enframement, stairs Type B; listed in 1849 city directory (No. 138) Charles Field; door late XIX cent., plate glass.

162, 164. 3-storied row houses, continuous brick façade; Greek Revival, pilastered doorways, stairs Type E; No. 164 listed in 1839 city directory (No. 142) Anthony Worthington and Asa Worthington, merchants; No. 162 in 1840 directory (No. 140) Frederick Mather, merchant; No. 164 has 4th story added, bracketed cornice; No. 162 has late XIX cent. stairs, ironwork; both have late XIX cent. doors, plate-glass windows.

168. 3-storied brick; listed in 1840 city directory (No. 146) Captain Benjamin Cooper, USN; story added, bracketed cornice, entrance lowered, "colonial" door, fence modern.

170. 3-storied brick, 4 bays wide; listed in 1840 city directory (No. 148) M. Marpilleroe, teacher of languages and mathematics; 2 stories added, bracketed cornice; balustrades on 1st-floor balconies; entrance lowered, plate glass, fire escape on front.

174, 176. 3-storied row houses, continuous brick façade; Greek Revival, pilastered doorways, stairs Type F; listed in 1844 city directory (No. 150) John T. Howard, merchant, and (No. 152) Isaac P. Frothingham, merchant; doorways have been altered, later doors, plate-glass windows.

178. 3-storied brick, similar to Nos. 174–76; listed in 1846 city directory (No. 154) Noah Ripley, oil merchant; entrance lowered.

260. 3-storied brick, originally faced Joralemon Street, similar to No. 37 Joralemon Street group; listed in 1845 city directory (No. 56 Jerolamon [*sic*]) Samuel M'Lean and Edward Philly; enlarged probably simultaneously with building of No. 162 Hicks Street group (1887) with new façade on Hicks Street having "Queen Anne" and Romanesque Revival details, including bay window on corner, scroll pediment doorway supported by clustered colonnettes, plate glass in windows.

286, 288, 290, 292. 3-storied row houses, continuous brick façade, each 2 bays wide, cornice on consoles, coupled windows, cornices on consoles over recessed entrances; No. 290 listed in 1856 city directory (No. 242) James Pike, fancy goods; No. 292 in 1857 city directory (No. 244) Thomas Dockum, real estate; Nos. 286, 288 in 1858 directory (No. 238) Alfred Windsor, and (No. 240) B. M. Field, dry goods; No. 288 modernized, entrance lowered; Nos. 286, 290 concrete railings to stairs; No. 292 modern ironwork.

302, 304, 306. 4-storied brick, each 2 bays wide, conceived as single composition, center one slightly advanced, pedimented, first story of stone given basement treatment; 1853 city directory lists No. 302 (No. 254) Alfred Clapp, and No. 306 (No. 258) D. B. and John C. Fuller, merchants; No. 304 listed in 1856 directory (No. 256) Thomas H. Green (also listed Thomas H. Greene), physician; No. 304 renovated in 1959, parapet replaces pediment, painted yellow.

308. 3-storied brick, corniced labels over windows; listed in 1846 city directory (n[ear] State) Henry U. Slipper (No. 260 in 1847 directory); 4th story and parapet later, entrance lowered, fire escape on front.

310. 3-storied brick, Greek Revival, pediment over door enframement with "Greek ears," stairs Type B; listed in 1846 city directory (n[ear] Joralemon?) George E. and John R. St. Felix (No. 262 in 1847 directory); plate glass in windows.

312. 4-storied brick, Greek Revival, corniced labels over windows (stripped), door enframement with "Greek ears," stairs Type B; listed in 1846 city directory (n[ear] State) Moses Allen (No. 264 in 1847 directory); later bracketed cornice, store in basement, fire escape on front.

east side

51. Similar to No. 155 Willow Street group; projecting stone stringer at 1st-floor level, interlacing muntins in top sash of arched dormer windows; listed in 1831 city directory (No. 47) Captain Ephraim Carning; in 1833 the home of Mott Bedell, shipmaster, who later resided at No. 11 Cranberry Street; doorway lowered, front wall painted gray.

57. 2-storied frame house; listed in 1826 city directory (No. 49) James H. Howland, merchant (No. 53 in 1829 directory); later mansard roof; stuccoed wall; store occupies 1st floor.

59. 2-storied frame house; listed in 1822 city directory (No. 51) John Rogers, cooper (No. 55 in 1829 directory); indicated composed only of front part on 1855 map; stuccoed, corner door modern.

125, 127, 129. 3-storied brownstones, high basement, cornices on brackets over windows, sash windows resembling French doors, stairs Type B; house on site of No. 129 listed in 1830 city directory (No. 111) John Coit; 1849 directory lists No. 125 (No. 107) A. K. and H. K. Corning, merchants, and No. 127 (No. 109) Peter Wyckoff; 4th stories added to Nos. 127, 129; details simplified, walls stuccoed; No. 129 has modern ironwork.

131, 135. 3-storied brownstone duplex in Gothic Revival style, hood molds over square-topped windows and Tudor-arched doorways with carving in spandrels, cast-iron traceried railings, coved cornice with bead-and-reel molding; listed in 1848 city directory (No. 113) Henry C. Bowen, merchant, and (No. 115) George F. Thomas, merchant; newel posts of No. 131 missing finials; posts of No. 135 late XIX cent., windows altered, top story added.

155. 3-storied brick; listed in 1830 city directory (No. 131) David Kimberly, merchant; top story, plate-glass windows and ironwork later.

165. 3-storied brick, Greek Revival, stone pilastered doorway, frieze windows in 3rd story entablature; listed in 1841 city directory (No. 137) Stephen Blake, merchant; late XIX cent. door, plate-glass windows, modern iron railing fence.

169, 171. 3-storied row houses, continuous brick façade, high basement; Greek Revival, pedimented doorways, enframements with "Greek ears," stairs Type E, contemporary iron fences; both listed in 1841 city directory (No. 141) J. B. Spelman, merchant, and (No. 143) David A. Bokee, merchant; No. 169 has bracketed cornice; No. 171 doorway altered; both have plate glass.

173, 175. 4-storied brick on high basements, built separately; Greek Revival, engaged Doric columns and entablature to recessed doorways; No. 175 listed in 1838 city directory (Hicks Street) Daniel Moran, teacher (No. 147 in 1839 directory); No. 173 in 1840 directory (No. 145) Joseph Dean, Captain W. H. Russell, and Edward G. Miller; cornice hoods over windows stripped, main-story windows filled in part way up from floor, doors late XIX cent. and modern, iron balustrades of entrance stairs late XIX cent., fences and cage posts modern.

271. 3-storied brick; listed in 1846 city directory (No. 225) William S. Tisdale; story added, late XIX cent. bracketed cornice, hoods and lintels over windows, pilastered doorway, ironwork and stone wall in front.

273, 275. 3-storied, continuous brick façade; No. 273 listed in 1844 city directory (c[orner] Jerolaman [*sic*]) James Rutherford, distiller (No. 227 in 1846 directory); No. 275 in 1846 directory (No. 229) Amanda Bidwell, widow; No. 275 has story added; both have entrances lowered, plate glass in windows.

281, 283. 3-storied row houses, continuous brick façade; Greek Revival, pilastered doorways, stairs Type E, contemporary fences; listed in 1848 city directory (No. 235) Edward H. Arthur, and (No. 237) H. B. Starr, merchant; entrance lowered of No. 281, fire escape on front.

289. 3-storied brick, Greek Revival, door enframement with "Greek ears," stairs Type E, contemporary fence; listed in 1845 city directory (n[ear] State) George S. Commover (No. 243 in 1847 directory); pediments over windows, plate glass.

301. 4-storied, high basement, segmented arched windows, listed in 1862 city directory (No. 253) Alfred Emanuel; stuccoed, entrance lowered.

Garden Place

(Supplementary illustrations nos. 65 and 66)

A STREET one block long connecting Joralemon and State streets, between Hicks and Henry streets, Garden Place came into being during or shortly after 1842, and was originally called Garden Street, because it occupies the site of the Philip Livingston garden. Part of the stone retaining wall separating the garden and orchard still forms the back fence of houses on the east side of the street, inclusive of Nos. 29–41. Today Garden Place is primarily a residential street of private ownership, its two apartment houses being relatively small and in scale with neighboring dwellings. Its buildings include a pre Civil War stable (No. 21) converted into an attractive home. With few exceptions its houses are nineteenth century. Much of the charm of Garden Place derives from the sycamore trees planted twenty years ago by the Langstaffs, residents at No. 39.

west side

10. 3-storied brick; listed in 1857 city directory (No. 3) Alfred H. Porter, grocer; "colonial" remodeling, including columned doorway with fanlight, modern ironwork.

28, 30, 32. 3-storied brownstones, Rence. Revival details, console cornices over openings; listed in 1856 city directory (No. 17) Charles H. Schneider, (No. 19) Henry G. Kopp, drugs, and (No. 21) William L. Kirby, broker; doorways altered; No. 32 has iron balustrades, Nos. 28, 30 have modern ironwork.

38. 3-storied brick, recessed doorway; listed in 1848 city directory (No. 29) Owen Byrne, liquor dealer; late XIX cent. changes include additional story with arched windows, hood molds, doorway, railings, plate glass.

east side

9, 11. 3-storied brick, corniced labels over openings, otherwise plain recessed doorways, stairs Type E; listed in 1845 city directory (n[ear] Jerolamon [*sic*]) Albert Putnam, shipmaster (No. 2 n[ear] Joralemon in 1846 directory, coal dealer), and Thomas M'Burney, slater (No. 4 n[ear] Joralemon in 1846 directory); later bracketed cornices, plate glass in windows and doors; molding over openings stripped from No. 11.

13. 3-storied brick, originally similar to neighbors; listed in 1845 city directory (n[ear] Jerolamon [*sic*]) Chandler Starr (No. 6 in 1846 directory); late XIX cent. cornice, hoods, doors, fence posts; railing modern.

15. 3-storied brick, low pedimented hoods over 1st-story openings, otherwise plain doorway, entrance stairs Type B; listed in 1846 city directory (No. 8) Miss Catherine Haff, John D. Hoag, merchant, and William Merrill, bookkeeper; plate-glass windows and glass in doors.

29, 31, 33. 3-storied row houses, continuous brick façade, drip molds over openings, entrances plain, stairs Type B; No. 29 listed in 1846 city directory (n[ear] Joralemon) Alfred S. Bond (No. 22 in 1847 directory); Nos. 31, 33 in 1847 directory (No. 24) Nathaniel Green, and (No. 26) Daniel Powers; mansard roof added to No. 33; drip molds stripped.

35. 3-storied brick, recessed entrance, stairs Type B; listed in 1850 city directory (No. 28) James Rutherford, distiller; later hoods over openings, modern door.

37, 39, 41. 3-storied row houses, continuous brick façade, openings plain except for corniced labels, stairs Type B; 1846 city directory lists No. 39 (n[ear] State) Henry S. Spencer (No. 32 n[ear] State in 1847 directory), and No. 41 (n[ear] State) Benjamin Smith, clerk (No. 34 in 1847 directory); No. 37 in 1847 directory (No. 30) B. F. Seaver; doors later; Nos. 37, 41 have bracketed cornices, plate-glass windows; No. 39 has been carefully restored, fire-engine plaque on wall, painted green, date 1845 (modern) in raised numerals on basement.

43. 3-storied brick, Greek Revival, pilastered doorway, stairs Type B; listed in 1848 city directory (No. 36) Charles Barnes; later bracketed cornice, plate-glass windows.

Henry Street

(Supplementary illustrations nos. 67–69)

THE SECOND of the two longest streets on Brooklyn Heights, Henry Street was designated John Street on the Jeremiah Lott map of 1816, at that time extending southward only as far as Waring Street (between Clark and Pierrepont, no longer existing).* No. 39 Henry Street is the only building in the area occupying the exact site of a structure depicted on the Lott map, and, although the front wall is of a later type of brickwork, part of the building may be the oldest surviving construction on the Heights. The present name of the street honors Thomas W. Henry, an early physician, and was attached before the publication of the first city directory in 1822.

The north end of Henry Street affords an axial view of the east towers of the Manhattan Bridge. The first few blocks in this vicinity are given over largely to industrial plants, dilapidated houses (a number of which were recently demolished), and squat commercial (eating and drinking) buildings; but Henry Street comes into its own after passing the Saint George Hotel. In the long block south of Clark Street are a number of interesting residences and two Gothic type churches, the First Presbyterian Church on the west side of the street built by W. B. Olmsted in 1846 and the German Lutheran Church on the east, the present façade of which dates from 1887. A little beyond the latter are four frame houses representing an original row of eleven that were built about 1828. Apparently otherwise of late Federal design, these houses have distyle porticoes with Greek Doric columns, that possibly are original; and, if so, this one detail constitutes a premature manifestation of the Greek Revival mode on Brooklyn Heights.

Only a few houses face Henry Street between Pierrepont and Joralemon streets. Stationed on the northeast corner of Remsen Street is Richard Upjohn's Church of the Pilgrims (1844–46), believed to be the first building in the Romanesque Revival style built in America. The appearance of the building, now become Our Lady of Lebanon, is marred by the removal of the spire on the tower, and the recent installation of windows unsympathetic to the architecture. Hunts Lane, opening off Henry Street a block south of the church, contains some charming two-storied brick carriage houses of the late nineteenth century, with upper floors converted into apartments.

The block between Joralemon and State streets is thickly built up with existing century-old houses.

31. First Presbyterian Church, Henry Street. Photograph by Edmund V. Gillon, Jr.

Close to our apartment. It
is now a Unitarian Church-

The numbering of the houses below Joralemon Street has been subject to several confusing changes; for instance, the old-style system, used throughout most of Brooklyn from the late 1820's until 1871, was not established on the west side of the block in question until 1847, and not on the east side until 1849. That adjacent houses may have been first listed in the city directories under totally unrelated numbers is explained by the fact that they were recorded in editions several years apart, and the numbering system had undergone changes in the meantime.

west side

114, 116. 4-storied, continuous brick façade, corniced labels; listed in 1848 city directory (No. 100) William Robbins, merchant, and (No. 102) R. R. Graves, merchant; modern "Renaissance" cornice; basement and 1st floor occupied by Candlelight Restaurant.

128. 3-storied brownstone, pediment on brackets over entrance, balustrade; listed in 1859 city directory (No. 106) Joseph Ely, dry goods.

130. 4-storied, segmented arched windows; listed in 1858 city directory (No. 108) Charles E. Crehan, butter; wall stuccoed, entrance lowered.

132, 134, 136, 138. 3-storied, continuous brick façade, plain doorways, stairs Type E, contemporary fences; listed in 1843 city directory (No. 110) Luther B. Wyman, (No. 112) William A. Morgan, dry goods, (No. 114) George Morgan, merchant, and (No. 116) Richard Thorne, merchant; later doors; No. 132 has later bracketed cornice, hoods over windows, modern railings; Nos. 134, 136, 138 have casement windows; Nos. 136, 138 have 3rd-story windows enlarged.

140. 4-storied; listed in 1832 city directory (No. 118) Hosea Webster; stuccoed, entrance lowered, window changes, fire escape on front.

142. 4-storied brownstone; house on site listed in 1829 city directory (No. 120) Henrietta Miller; present building probably dates from late 1850's; stuccoed, entrance lowered.

144. 4-storied; listed in 1856 city directory (No. 122) Joseph M. Hager, music teacher (in appendix, received too late for regular insertion); stuccoed, entrance lowered, ironwork modern.

146. 3-storied brick, high basement; listed in 1843 city directory (No. 124) Abernijah Underhill; stuccoed, metal casement windows, entrance lowered and embellished with sculptured reliefs, brick fence.

148. 3-storied brick, high basement; listed in 1840 city directory (No. 126) Rev. Lawson Carter; modern brick facing, entrance lowered, metal sash windows.

150. 3-storied brick, high basement; Greek Revival, pilastered doorway; listed in 1830 city directory (No. 128) Philip Brasher; bay window over doorway, cornice hoods over windows, plate glass, modern railing.

222, 224, 226. 3-storied, continuous brick façade, corniced labels over openings, doorways otherwise plain, stairs Type B; Nos. 222, 224 listed in 1851 city directory, (No. 144) J. Borciaus, merchant, and (No. 146) Charles Ely, merchant; No. 226 in 1855 directory (No. 148) William Holworthy, coffee; bracketed hoods over doors later; Nos. 222, 226 have 4th floor added; No. 222 modern railings and fence; No. 226 entrance lowered; Nos. 224, 226 plate glass.

228. 3-storied brick, corniced labels over openings; listed in 1851 city directory (No. 148) Edward Lambert, merchant (No. 150 in 1852 directory); 4th story added, entrance lowered, plate glass in windows, ironwork modern.

242, 244, 246, 248. 3-storied brick row houses, built separately; Greek Revival, pilastered doorways (Nos. 242, 248) and entrance steps Type F; 1846 city directory lists No. 244 (No. 206) John Brouwer, pres. ER Ins. Co., N. Y. (No. 158 in 1849 directory), and No. 246 (No. 208) Joshua Atkins, Jr. (No. 160 in 1849 directory); No. 242 listed in 1848 directory (No. 204) James R. Jewett (No. 156 in 1849 directory); and No. 248 listed in 1849 directory (No. 162) William Faber, merchant; Nos. 242, 246 have later bracketed cornices; Nos. 244, 246 have late XIX cent. doorways and stairs, others later doors only; all have plate glass in windows.

250. 3-storied brick, Greek Revival, door enframement with "Greek ears"; listed in 1848 city directory (No. 212) Major L. Capers, USN (No. 164 in 1849 directory); doors later, iron balustrade, plate glass, mansard roof.

252. 3-storied brick; listed in 1848 city directory (No. 214) Sarah Mills, widow, boarding house (No. 166 in 1849 directory); late XIX cent. console cornice, window frames with frieze and cornices above, plate glass, console doorway, iron balustrade.

254, 256, 258. 3-storied brick row houses, built separately, corniced labels over windows; No. 254 listed in 1837 city directory (n[ear] Joralemon) David Stanford (No. 168 n[ear] Joralemon in 1846 directory); No. 258 in 1846 directory (n[ear] Joralemon) Jeanette Denton, widow

(No. 172 in 1847 directory); No. 256 in 1848 directory (No. 218) Nicholas Plass, broker (No. 170 in 1849 directory); 4th stories added, entrances lowered, façade painted yellow, plate glass in windows, concrete fence in front.

260. 3-storied brick, high basement; Greek Revival, recessed pilastered doorway, stairs Type C (?); listed in 1843 city directory (n[ear] Joralemon) Ezra Lewis, merchant (No. 174 in 1847 directory); later doors, cage posts and iron railings are modern "colonial," plate glass.

262. 3-storied brick, Greek Revival, pilastered doorway, stairs Type B; listed in 1845 city directory (n[ear] Jerolamon [*sic*]) R. H. Green, broker (No. 176 in 1847 directory); doors later, plate glass in windows.

264. 3-storied brick; listed in 1844 city directory (No. 210) Nathaniel Putnam (n[ear] Joralemon in 1846 directory, No. 178 in 1847 directory); end of XIX cent. pilastered doorway, railing and stonework in front, plate glass.

266. 3-storied brick; listed in 1849 city directory (No. 180) Robert Aborn; later pedimented overdoor on consoles above entrance, stuccoed façade and stuccoed walls replacing balustrades, plate glass.

268. 4-storied brick, corniced labels over windows; listed in 1848 city directory (No. 230) N. Taylor (No. 182 in 1849 directory); entrance lowered, fire escape on front.

270. 3-storied brick; Greek Revival door enframement with "Greek ears"; listed in 1848 city directory (No. 232) Samuel Sweatzer, broker (No. 184 in 1849 directory); late XIX cent. changes include bracketed cornice, hood molds, ironwork and some "Romanesque" brownstone.

272. 3-storied brick; listed in 1849 city directory (No. 186) Samuel Williams; later bracketed cornice; entrance lowered, "colonial" doorway.

274. 4-storied, cornices on brackets over openings; listed in 1858 city directory (No. 188) Daniel St. Amant, merchant; entrance lowered, concrete and iron fence modern.

276. 4-storied; listed in 1852 city directory (No. 190) Benjamin Blossom, merchant; stuccoed, entrance lowered, fire escape on front.

278. 3-storied brownstone, cornices over windows, pediment on consoles over doorway, brownstone fence; listed in 1851 city directory (No. 192) John Peck, commission merchant.

280, 282. 3-storied row houses, continuous Flemish-bond brick façade; No. 280 listed in 1837 city directory (No. 206) George Wood, counsellor-at-law (retains same number through 1850, n[ear] State); No. 282 listed in 1839 directory (No. 208) John Peck, commission merchant (indicated last house west side between Joralemon and State in 1840 house guide, No. 196 in 1849 directory); No. 282 has late XIX cent. bracketed cornice; No. 280 has mansard roof; both have entrances lowered.

east side

***29.** 2-storied, 1st frame, 2nd brick, extremely narrow; listed in 1830 city directory (No. 35) Elizabeth White.

***89.** 5-storied brick; listed in 1829 city directory (No. 75) George A. Hicks, grocer and tea dealer; stuccoed, store 1st story.

119, 121. 3-storied brownstones, Romanesque cornice, stairs Type B; listed in 1849 city directory (No. 103) George Cornell, and (No. 105) Hiram N. Peck, merchant; No. 121 has 4th story added, entrance lowered; both have plate-glass windows.

133. 3-storied brick, high basement; Greek Revival, pilastered recessed doorway; listed in 1840 city directory (No. 109) Abraham Crist, lawyer; later console cornice, doors, balustrade railing, plate glass.

135. 3-storied; listed in 1844 city directory (No. 111) Thomas Clark, merchant; synthetic stone façade, metal casement windows, entrance lowered.

137, 139, 141, 143. 3-storied clapboarded frame row houses, high brick basements, survivors of row of 11 wooden houses extending to corner Love Lane; carved doorway enframements, distyle Greek Doric porticoes; No. 143 listed in 1829 city directory (No. 119) Mrs. E. Gregory; 1830 directory lists No. 137 (No. 113) Benjamin Talbot, merchant, which became the home of Cyrus P. Smith in 1834 (mayor of Brooklyn in 1839), and No. 139 (No. 115) Amasa Wright; No. 141 listed in 1831 directory (No. 117) William R. Dwight; changes include late XIX cent. bay windows over porticoes of Nos. 137, 143, bracketed cornices of Nos. 141, 143, lowering of entrance of No. 139, walls of Nos. 137, 139, and 143 covered with asbestos or synthetic shingles, and plate-glass windows in all.

253, 255, 257. 3-storied brick row houses, bracketed gables; houses on site listed in 1849 city directory (No. 153) Francis Vinton, D. D., rector Grace Church, (No. 155) Charles I. Coggill, merchant, and (No. 157) Henry A. Swift, merchant; details and fences late XIX cent.; No. 253 has some "Renaissance" details, bay window and doorway.

259. 3-storied Flemish-bond brickwork; listed in 1833 city directory (No. 197) Alfred Benson, commission merchant (No. 187 in 1834 directory); present details late XIX cent.; rear wing (brick) reported moved from house on Remsen Street.

261, 263. 3-storied duplex, continuous brick façade, Greek Revival, corniced labels over windows, pilastered doorways, stairs Type B, note unusual contemporary banisters and iron railing and fence of No. 261; listed in 1849 city directory (No. 161) F. A. Spies, and (No. 163) C. Poppenhusen; No. 263 has mansard roof, "Queen Anne" bay window over doorway, doorway altered, modern ironwork.

265, 267. 3-storied row houses, continuous brick façade, stairs Type B; No. 265 listed in 1844 city directory (No. 209) Alfred R. Mount, merchant (No. 213 in 1846 directory, No. 165 in 1849 directory); No. 267 listed in 1848 directory (No. 215 b[etween] State & Joralemon) Edward Dunham, merchant (No. 167 b[etween] State & Joralemon in 1849 directory); No. 265 has later bracketed cornice, doorway altered; No. 267 has pedimented console doorway, plate glass in windows, modern ironwork.

273, 275. 3-storied row houses, continuous brick façade, corniced labels over windows; listed in 1849 city directory (No. 173) James Nesbitt, and (No. 175) Frederick Vietor, merchant; door frames later, entrances lowered, modern fences, plate glass; No. 275 has mansard roof.

277. 4-storied; listed in 1849 city directory (No. 177) Mrs. White, widow; stuccoed, entrance lowered, plate glass, modern ironwork.

279. 3-storied brick, corniced labels over voids; listed in 1841 city directory (n[ear] Joralemon) George F. Duckwitz (No. 179 b[etween] State and Joralemon in 1849 directory); story added, entrance lowered, plate glass, ironwork modern.

285. 3-storied brick corniced lintels over windows; listed in 1847 city directory (No. 185) James Nesmith, merchant; console cornice, fire escape on front, entrance lowered, cement fence.

287, 289, 291. 3-storied, continuous brick façade, entrance stairs Type D (ironwork like No. 109 State Street group); Nos. 289, 291 listed in 1839 city directory (No. 201) Samuel Jackson USN, and (No. 203) Jean Jacques Merian, merchant (No. 191 [John J. Merrian] in 1849 directory); No. 287 listed in 1840 city directory (n[ear] State) Benjamin J. Cahoone (indicated north side of S. Jackson in 1840 house guide); No. 287 has contemporary fence, later bracketed cornice; No. 289 has mansard roof; Nos. 287, 289 doorways and stairs later treatment; No. 291 entrance lowered, cornices over openings, modern fence.

295, 297. 3-storied brownstones, continuous façade; bracketed cornice, cornices over windows, pediments on brackets over doors, stairs Type B; house on site of No. 295 listed in 1847 city directory (No. 195) Henry Everit; No. 297 listed in 1852 directory (No. 197) E. T. H. Gibson; stairs of No. 295 later.

301. 3-storied brick; listed in 1833 city directory (c[orner] Henry and State) Richard White, merchant (indicated on northeast corner in 1840 house guide); story added with late XIX cent. bracketed cornice, bay window on corner, ironwork; entrance lowered.

Monroe Place

(Supplementary illustration no. 70 and frontispiece)

THE WIDEST street on Brooklyn Heights, and, except for College Place, the only one having the odd house numbers on the west and the even ones on the east side of the block, Monroe Place also bears the distinction of being the only street retaining the old-style numbering system, elsewhere abandoned in 1871. Monroe Place came into being during the early 1830's, and was named after James Monroe, fifth president of the United States, who, in 1831, ended his days in New York City in impoverished exile from his native Virginia. The British fort on Brooklyn Heights during the American Revolution stood at the junction of Monroe Place and Pierrepont Street. Love Lane once cut through this end, continuing to Fulton Street; and several houses in the vicinity are without a single right-angled corner, because of their alignment to the lane (Nos. 44, 46). The row of buildings on the east side begins and ends with mid-nineteenth-century brownstone churches designed by Minard Lafever, the *Church of the Restoration (1848) at Clark Street, and the Church of the Saviour (1844) at Pierrepont Street. Also noteworthy are the iron basket urns set on pedestals at the foot of the entrance stairs to No. 46, this pair of urns being a unique survivor of what was once a prevalent feature on the Heights. Connecting two cross streets, Monroe Place is disturbed by very little traffic.

32. Entrance stairs to No. 46 Monroe Place. Only complete specimen of "Type D" surviving on the Heights.

west side

1. 3-storied brick; listed in 1852 city directory, Samuel C. West, commission merchant; mansard roof added, details altered, entrance lowered, plate glass in windows.

3. 3-storied brick; Greek Revival, scroll pediment over doorway, entrance stairs Type E; listed in 1849 city directory, Augustus Studwell, lumber; later 2nd-story bay window, door, plate glass.

5. Probably originally similar to No. 3; listed in 1849 city directory, D. Anderson, brown and blue stone yard; late XIX cent. doorway and ironwork, walls stuccoed, plate glass in windows.

7. 3-storied brick, entrance stairs Type B; listed in 1849 city directory, Issac Harris, shipmaster; stripped of details, doors of later period, plate glass in windows.

9. 3-storied brick; listed in 1845 city directory, Joshua Atkins, merchant;

late XIX cent. doorway, stairs, ironwork and stonework, bracketed cornice, plate-glass windows.

11. 3-storied brick; listed in 1842 city directory, David F. Atwater, physician, and George M. Atwater, merchant; no details of interest, floor added, entrance lowered.

13, 15. 3-storied row houses, continuous brownstone façade, bracketed cornice, hoods over windows, cornices on carved consoles over doorways, contemporary iron railings and fences; listed in 1851 city directory, No. 13, Richard R. Field, and, No. 15, Edward S. Dennis, shipmaster; arched "colonial" doorways.

17. 4-storied brick; listed in 1845 city directory as home of Mary, Boardman, George, Jonathan and Samuel Howard; stripped of details, stuccoed, entrance lowered.

19. 3-storied brick, Greek Revival, pilastered doorway, stairs Type E; listed in 1845 city directory (n[ear] Love Lane) Edward S. Howard, merchant (No. 19 in 1847 directory); later bracketed cornice, "colonial" recessed door, plate-glass windows.

27. 3-storied brick; listed in 1844 city directory (n[ear] Clark) Edmund Blunt, U. S. coast surveyor (No. 27 in 1848 directory); present appearance similar to No. 11, story added, given casement windows, entrance lowered "colonial" details.

29, 31. Brick houses, at present 4-storied; one listed in 1838 city directory without street number, John Graham, white lead works, shown in 1840 house guide to be on west side, north of W. J. Cornell residence; No. 31 listed in 1850 city directory as home of Joseph P. Wickham, dry goods; No. 29 in 1852 directory, Daniel C. Robbins, druggist; stuccoed, entrances lowered; No. 29 has late XIX cent. bracketed cornice, No. 31 has modern metal casement windows.

33. 3-storied brick; listed in 1839 city directory (n[ear] Pierpont [*sic*]) Whitehead J. Cornell, who lived here until 1846; 1847 directory lists Julia Cornell, widow of W. J. (Monroe Pl. n[ear] Pierrepont); 1848 directory gives the name Juliet Cornell, widow of W. J., with present street number; stripped of details, entrance lowered.

east side

***8.** 3-storied brick, plain doorway, entrance stairs Type B; listed in 1848 city directory, William Kent, merchant; mansard roof added, details stripped, casement windows main story.

10. House listed in 1848 city directory, William H. Allen, shipmaster; in 1936 converted into apartment building showing no feature of original architecture.

33. Side door of No. 107 State Street (No. 60 Sidney Place).

12, 14. 3-storied row houses having continuous brick façade, entrance stairs Type B; No. 12 listed in 1847 city directory (Monroe Place) George Coggeshall, shipmaster (No. 12 in 1848 directory); No. 14 listed in 1849 directory William R. Phelps, clerk; finials missing from newel posts; late XIX cent. details including bay window over doorway of No. 14, plate glass in windows.

18, 20. 3-storied brownstone row houses similar to Nos. 13, 15; listed in 1854 city directory, No. 18, George H. Studwell, merchant, and No. 20, Augustus Baldwin, clothing; No. 18 has added mansard roof, hood mold over entrance altered, main-floor windows now casement; No. 20 has been stripped of details, walls stuccoed.

36. 4-storied; listed in 1851 city directory, No. 36, Rev. Henry S. Wilkins; details obliterated, stuccoed, entrance lowered.

44, 46. 2-storied row houses, continuous Flemish-bond brick façade, high brownstone basement; Greek Revival, Doric stone doorway, steps Type D with fine wrought-iron railings, basket urns capped with pineapples set on paneled stone pedestals, contemporary fence with cresting of anthemions (No. 46 only); plans of houses slightly irregular shape because lots aligned to former continuation of Love Lane; No. 44 listed in 1835 city directory (n[ear] Love-lane) J. Jewett (street number given in 1851 directory, John Jewett, oil cloth manufacturer); No. 46 in 1836 city directory (no street number given) Amos P. Stanton (n[ear] Pierpont [*sic*] in 1838 directory, street number given in 1851 directory, Stanton identified as merchant, resided here until 1861); both have 3rd stories added in plain brickwork; No. 44 renovated for apartments, details altered, entrance lowered; No. 46 has 3rd-story front heightened in plain brickwork, top windows arched, bracketed cornice, plate glass in windows, doorway modified.

Sidney Place

(Supplementary illustrations nos. 71 and 72)

SHOWN nameless and extending only a little below Livingston Street on the 1819 Trustees Map, on Hooker's Pocket Plan of Brooklyn (1827), and also on Isaac Ludlam's survey of the Pierrepont property (1831) this street was called Monroe (the present Monroe Place did not exist at the time); but the title was changed within the next few years by George Wood, borough attorney, to memorialize Sir Philip

Sidney, the sixteenth-century English statesman and author. In the Brooklyn city directories prior to 1850 the spelling of "Sidney" sometimes was given with a "y" and sometimes with an "i," the two letters also being used interchangeably in the surname of the British knight.

Sidney Place is a wide, short street, running from Joralemon to State Street, and is on an axis with Monroe Place, which is three blocks to the north. On the north corner of Livingston Street stands the Church of Saint Charles Borromeo (*ca.* 1870), and on the south corner its rectory (1928) adjoining the parish school (1916). The row houses on the east side south of Livingston Street, built simultaneously in 1845, are set back from the sidewalk with front yards inside iron fences, and, although variously altered, still present a pleasing effect. No. 35 is the best preserved of the row, except for its later doorway, the original form of which is to be seen in the recessed entrance of No. 49. Nos. 18 and 20 Sidney Place date from the 1830's, the former possessing a noble Greek Doric doorway. The side door to the last house on the west side of the street (No. 107 State) is embellished with an anthemion motif from a design by Minard Lafever, architect of Packer Collegiate Institute a few blocks away, and one of the chief exponents of the Greek Revival mode of building in America.

west side

2. Shallow 3½-storied brick, north wall continuous brickwork with façade of No. 120 Joralemon Street group; listed in 1846 city directory (Joralemon c[orner] Sydney Place) Daniel Chauncey, builder (No. 2 Sydney in 1849 directory); late XIX cent. "stick style" entrance vestibule with bay window above, doorway itself of early XIX cent. type similar to that of No. 135 Joralemon Street opposite, said to have come from a frame house on the site of the Towers Hotel; cast-iron fence late XIX cent.

8, 10, 12, 14, 16. 3-storied row houses, continuous brick façade, plain recessed doorways, entrance stairs Type E; 1845 city directory lists first three (n[ear] Jerolamon [*sic*]), No. 8, William Newell (No. 4 in 1848 directory), No. 10, William

Hull (No. 6 in 1848 directory), No. 12, D. C. Clark, merchant (No. 8 in 1848 directory); similarly designated in the 1845 directory are Albert Gates, jeweler, E. C. Hamilton, merchant, and Samuel R. Kelly, merchant, but names do not appear in the 1848 directory where street numbers are first used for this group; entrances lowered of Nos. 8 and 16; No. 8 has 4th floor added, No. 10 console heading over front door, modern railing.

18. 3-storied brick on high basement; Greek Revival, recessed doorway enframed by Doric columns and entablature, corniced labels over windows; listed in 1838 city directory (Sidney Place) Thomas Kirk, U. S. weigher (indicated north side of Brownson in 1840 house guide); house number first appears in 1848 directory (No. 14) Elizabeth M. Jannet (listed as residing on Sidney Place year previously); 3 floors added, bracketed cornice, later doors, plate-glass windows.

20. 3-storied brick originally 3 bays wide; listed in 1838 city directory (Sydney Place) John Brownson, merchant (n[ear] State in 1845 directory, No. 16 in 1847 directory); extension with bay window added on south side, also 4th story with bracketed cornice; entrance lowered.

44, 46, 48, 50, 52. 3-storied row houses, continuous brick façade, low gabled hoods over plain recessed doorways, stairs Type E; Nos. 44, 46, 48 listed in 1843 city directory (No. 38) Matthew Wilson, artist, (No. 40) H. D. Sharp, merchant, and (No. 42) Charles Davidson; 1844 directory lists Nos. 50, 52, (No. 44) Albert G. Allen, merchant, and (No. 46) James Robinson; Nos. 44, 50 have later bracketed cornices; Nos. 46, 50 late XIX cent. railings; No. 52 completely renovated, window pattern changed, entrance lowered.

54. 3-storied brick, hood-molds over windows, coved cornice, probably similar to house on corner, No. 107 State Street; listed in 1847 city directory (Sidney Place) Zebeziah Ingalls, merchant (No. 48 in 1848 directory); entrance lowered, details stripped, casement windows 1st story, others plate glass.

east side

31, 33, 35, 37, 39, 41, 43, 45, 47, 49. 3-storied row houses, high basement, continuous brick façade; Greek Revival, plain recessed doorways (No. 49 alone has original pilastered inner doors), stairs Type E (Nos. 35, 43, 49), contemporary fences (Nos. 35, 37, 45, 47 and 49); No. 37 listed in 1846 city directory (n[ear] Livingston) C. P. Baldwin (No. 35 n[ear] Livingston in 1849 directory); No. 39 in 1847 directory (Sydney Place) G. A. Clark (J. A. Clark, No. 37 in 1849 directory); 1848 directory lists

No. ,31 (n[ear] Livingston) John Cowenhoven (No. 29 in 1850 directory), and No. 35 (n[ear] Livingston) Emery H. Penniman (No. 33 Sydney in 1850); 1849 directory lists No. 33 (No. 31) Andrew Smith, No. 41 (No. 39) James Robinson, and No. 43 (No. 41) Joseph Lovell, lawyer; 1850 directory lists No. 45 (No. 43) Herman Livingston, custom house, and No. 47 (No. 45) Francis Glos, merchant; No. 49 listed in 1851 directory (No. 47) R. H. Hopkins, merchant; No. 31 (now convent St. Charles Borromeo) has later mansard roof, entrance lowered, plate glass; No. 33 has "colonial" frieze and cornice, "Romanesque" doorway, plate glass; No. 35 later door; No. 37 stripped, plate glass; No. 39 has floor added, entrance lowered, stuccoed, plate glass; No. 41 has later pediment on consoles over doorway, railings, plate glass; No. 43 has bracketed cornice, plate glass; No. 45 stripped, entrance lowered, plate glass; No. 47 has late XIX cent. railings, plate glass; and No. 49 (best preserved of last four) has later outer doors, plate glass.

Clinton Street

(Supplementary illustrations nos. 73–75)

NAMED after De Witt Clinton, governor of the State of New York after 1817, Clinton Street is the easternmost and the latest of Brooklyn Heights streets of north to south orientation. Some of the handsomest public and semipublic buildings in the area are adjacent to Clinton Street. It begins at the junction of Fulton and Tillary streets. In the first block are the two Crescent Athletic Club buildings, the older one (currently being demolished), in the Saracenic style, constructed on the east side of the street in 1894, and the later one, on the northwest corner of Pierrepont, built by the architect Frank Freeman in 1906. Freeman also built the Brooklyn Savings Bank on the northeast corner in 1893. Opposite these two buildings are the Long Island Historical Society and the former Brooklyn Trust Company, built, respectively, by George B. Post in 1878 and York and Sawyer in 1915. Behind the Historical Society, facing Clinton Street, stands Minard Lafever's Church of the Holy Trinity, constructed in the Gothic Revival style in 1844–47, its brownstone details now looking rather the worse

34. Church of the Holy Trinity, corner of Clinton and Montague streets. From Minard Lafever, The Architectural Instructor, *New York, 1856.*

for more than a century of weathering, and its spire gone. On the southeast corner of Remsen is the First Church of Brooklyn (Presbyterian) (1850), and a block beyond is the impressive polychromed stonework façade of Saint Anne's P. E. Church, built in the Venetian Gothic manner by Renwick and Sands in 1867–69. Two tall buildings on Clinton deserve mention: one is the Romanesque Revival Franklin Trust Company Building (1891) across from the Church of the Holy Trinity, and the other the Insurance Building, with modern gothic details, at Joralemon Street facing Saint Anne's Church. The balance of Clinton Street, down to State, is devoted to groups of mid-nineteenth-century row houses.

west side

140, 142. 3-storied brick row houses, 2-part compositions, bracketed gables, elaborately modeled iron hoods over openings (those 1st story of No. 142 modern castings because of former conversion into grocery), survivors of a row of five similar houses; listed in 1855 city directory (No. 68) Bern L. Budd and Elias Trivett, druggists, and (No. 70) Ludlow Thomas, broker; modern iron railings.

148. 3-storied brick, high basement; listed in 1848 city directory (No. 74) S. S. Guy, physician; later additional story, entrance lowered, changes to windows including casements 1st-floor front.

150. Originally similar to No. 148; listed in 1847 city directory (No. 76) Mrs. S. Oakley, widow; story added, entrance lowered, ground- and 1st-floor wall recessed, stuccoed, blind arch to center window 2nd floor.

154. 3-storied brick; listed in 1845 city directory (n[ear] Livingston) Richard J. Dodge, merchant (No. 80 in 1847 directory); bracketed cornice, plate-glass windows, entrance lowered.

156, 158. 3-storied row houses, continuous brick façade; Greek Revival, low pediments over windows, pilastered doorways, stairs Type B; listed in 1847 city directory (No. 82) James O. Lloyd, merchant, and (n[ear] Livingston) Samuel R. Kelly, commission merchant (No. 84 in 1848 directory); No. 156 has late XIX cent. mansard roof, doors and balustrades; No. 158 has "colonial" doorway; plate-glass windows in both.

160, 162. 3-storied row houses, continuous brick façade, originally similar to adjoining houses on north; No. 162 listed in 1845 city directory (n[ear] Livingston) Edward Bridge, merchant (op[posite] Schermerhorn in 1846 directory, No. 88 in 1847 directory); No. 160 in 1846 directory (n[ear] Livingston) Esther Jackson, widow (No. 86 in 1847 directory); No. 160 has bracketed cornice, later door, balustrade; No. 162 entrance lowered; both plate-glass windows.

164, 166, 168. 3-storied row houses, continuous brick façade, high basement, Greek Revival, pilastered doorways, stairs Type B, contemporary fence (No. 168 only); No. 166 listed in 1846 city directory (n[ear] State) James Moore (No. 92 in 1848 directory); No. 164 in 1847 directory (op[posite] Schermerhorn) James Trip (James Trippe, druggist, No. 90 in 1848 directory); No. 168 in 1848 directory (No. 94) Silas Ludlam, city surveyor; plate glass in windows; No. 164 has modern ironwork; fire escape on front of No. 168.

170. 4-storied brick; listed in 1846 directory (n[ear] State) Isaac Otis, grocer (No. 96 in 1847 directory); story added, entrance lowered, stuccoed.

172. 3-storied brick; listed in 1846 city directory (n[ear] State) L. Ballard (No. 98 in 1848 directory, furrier); bracketed cornice, entrance lowered, casement windows.

174. 3-storied brick; listed in 1847 city directory (No. 100) John Dimon, builder; late XIX cent. bracketed cornice and other details, stairs and ironwork, plate glass.

178. 3-storied brick, similar to No. 174; listed in 1848 city directory (No. 102) Lyman Sears, merchant; entrance lowered.

180. 3-storied brick, plain recessed doorway, stairs Type E; listed in 1848 city directory (No. 104) Thomas Godet, M.D.B.; door and plate-glass windows later.

182, 184. 3-storied row houses, continuous brick wall, plain recessed doorways; both listed in 1848 city directory (No. 106) Thomas Sinclair, physician, and (c[orner] State) H. L. Benjamin, physician (No. 108 c[orner] State in 1849 directory); door and railings of No. 182 late XIX cent.; No. 184 entrance lowered, casement windows 1st floor; plate glass elsewhere, both have bracketed cornices.

east side

***29.** 4-storied; listed in 1848 city directory (No. 25) G. L. Willard, commission merchant; later bracketed cornice, front extension including store in basement and 1st floor.

31. 3-storied brick; listed in 1842

35. Doorway to No. 24 Middagh Street.

city directory (n[ear] Pierrepont) Martha Middagh, widow (No. 27 in 1847 directory); 1st floor made into store, plate glass in windows.

133. 3-storied brick; listed in 1851 city directory (No. 75) Edward Pumetta; later heavy bracketed cornice, bay window on north flank, console hood over doorway, formerly also over windows (like neighbors) now replaced by lintels with urns in low relief in end panels.

135, 137, 139. 3-storied row houses, continuous brick façade, high basement, stairs Type B and contemporary fence (No. 137 only); 1850 city directory lists No. 137 (No. 79) Dan Marvin; 1851 directory lists No. 135 (No. 77) Ten Eyck Stutphen, merchant, and No. 139 (No. 81) Edward Pumetta; later doors, plate glass; No. 135 has modern railing; No. 139 has concrete railing and fence.

141, 143, 145, 147. 3-storied brick with continuous façade, recessed doorways plain except for simple scrolled heading, bracket cornice; listed in 1853 city directory, No. 141 (No. 83) John B. Flagg, glass manufacturer, No. 143 (No. 85) E. Clapp, commission merchant, No. 145 (No. 87) C. F. Leavitt, agent, and No. 147 (No. 89) A. Taylor; No. 141 alone retains doorway, though door and ironwork are later; others have entrances lowered.

151. 3-storied brick, plain except for cornices over openings, originally similar to No. 153 group; listed in 1851 city directory (No. 93) Philip Van Valkenburgh, merchant; bracketed cornice, later railing and stucco work in front, plate-glass windows.

153, 155, 157. 3-storied row houses, continuous brick façade, plain except for cornices over openings, entrance stairs Type E; No. 155 listed in 1846 city directory (n[ear] State) Frederick Hewett, shipmaster (No. 97 in 1848 directory); 1848 directory lists No. 153 (No. 95) A. Austin Hall, merchant, and No. 157 (No. 99) William Evans, merchant tailer; No. 155 has entrance lowered; all have plate-glass windows.

159, 161, 163. 3-storied row houses, high basements, Gothic Revival, drip molds over openings (stripped), doorways have Tudor arches; listed in 1849 city directory (No. 101) Lewis D. Bulkley, merchant, (No. 103) John Fish, and (No. 105) Richard Bainbridge, merchant; bracketed cornice, doors later, plate glass, walls stuccoed, concrete railings and fences.

165. 3-storied brick, similar to No. 159 group only has Greek Revival pilastered doorway, cornices over windows; listed in 1849 city directory (No. 107) J. M. Stockwell, merchant; later ironwork and stucco walls in front, plate-glass windows.

167. 3-storied brick, Gothic Revival, similar to No. 159 group, retains tracery cast-iron fences, railings, clustered-colonnette newel posts crowned by pinnacles with crockets; listed in 1849 city directory No. 109 c[orner] State) Benjamin S. Lyman, dentist; hood molds over windows stripped, plate glass installed, doors later, bracketed cornice.

Middagh Street

(Supplementary illustration no. 76)

ORIGINALLY having the first and later the second name of Aert Middagh, this street was entitled either by John Middagh (son of Aert) or by the Hicks brothers after their maternal ancestors. Gabriel Furman recorded the existence of eighteen dwellings, three school houses, three stables, one carpenter shop, and a fire-engine house on Middagh Street in 1821. A modern description of the street would bear striking similarities to the Furman account. The west end has been cleared of structures because of the Brooklyn-Queens Expressway that passes underneath. The next two blocks exhibit a number of frame houses built during the 1820's, and a few later Greek Revival brick residences. The handsomest and best preserved example in this group is the Federal residence, No. 24. Of special interest is old District School #8 on the north side of the street at the crest of the hill, built of brick laid in common bond in 1846, having a T-plan, the first of its three stories given a high basement treatment with arches left open along the flanks. A twentieth-century building on Hicks Street south of Middagh Street has taken over the functions of the public school (still designated #8), and the early-nineteenth-century building has become the Assumption Parochial School.

south side

24. 2½-storied clapboarded frame house on Flemish-bond brick basement; dormer windows in curb roof; Federal style, leaded glass in transom and side lights of front door flanked by Ionic colonnettes, rustication, elaborately carved blocks to frame; arched window, half-lunettes to garret on west flank, blind windows centered on 1st and 2nd stories; listed in 1829 city directory (No. 42) Eugene Boisselet; originally had porch across back of house; carriage house on Willow Street connected to residence by screen board wall; fence and railings to front stoop are modern.

26. 3-storied brick, Flemish bond; listed in 1829 city directory (No. 44) Phebe Burtis; entrance lowered.

28. 3-storied frame house; listed in 1829 city directory (No. 46) John M'Manus, shipmaster; modern alterations, walls covered composition shingles, garage in basement.

30. 3-storied frame house; listed in 1824 city directory (No. 45) widow of Benjamin Smith (No. 47 in 1825, No. 48 in 1829 directory); pilastered Greek Revival entrance at street level; wall covered with asphalt shingles.

56. 2½-storied frame house on high basement; listed in 1829 city directory (No. 66) Robert Philips and Joseph Haggert, blacksmiths; mid XIX cent. remodeled Greek Revival style, with distyle Doric portico.

north side

23. 3-storied, brick façade continuous with south flank of No. 15 Willow Street; similar doorway; entrance steps Type E; listed in 1834 city directory (No. 43) Henry and Thomas Everit; doorway badly weathered.

25. Small 2-storied frame house; listed in 1824 city directory (No. 46) Michael Trapple, laborer (No. 50 in 1825, No. 45 in 1829 directory); stuccoed, entrance lowered.

27. 3-storied frame house, shingled, high basement; listed in 1829 city directory (No. 47) Norman Olmstead; late XIX cent. bracketed cornice.

29. Similar to No. 27; listed in 1830 city directory (No. 49) Andrew Hebard, engineer.

31, 33. 2-storied frame duplex; No. 31 listed in 1847 city directory (No. 51) Davies & Jones, paint store; No. 33 listed in 1848 directory (No. 53) William Heck, hairdresser; covered with stucco, windows of No. 31 changed.

55. 2-storied frame house, clapboarded, high basement of Flemish bond brickwork, 3 bays wide plus extension east end with elliptical windows over service passage; listed in 1829 city directory (No. 71) John Laidlaw, teacher; perhaps same house referred to under same name in 1826 directory (No. 28), in 1823–25 directories (No. 26), and in 1822 directory (No. 24).

57. 3-storied frame house on high basement of Flemish-bond brickwork; listed in 1834 city directory (No. 73) John G. Kirk, commission merchant; late XIX cent. bracketed cornice; entrance lowered, walls covered with asphalt shingles.

59. 3-storied frame, 4 bays wide, clapboarded; listed in 1832 city directory (No. 75) William Rog, professor of Hebrew; late XIX cent. bracketed cornice.

Cranberry Street

HAVING an imaginative name given it by the Hicks brothers, Cranberry Street, like Middagh Street, extends from Columbia Heights to Fulton Street, and once continued eastward prior to the laying out of Parkes Cadman Plaza. Gabriel Furman counted fifteen dwellings and one carpenter shop on Cranberry Street in 1821. From about 1836 until 1853 the end of Colonnade Row, facing Columbia Street, came to the northeast corner of Cranberry Street; and across on the southeast corner stood the Greek Revival duplex housing Dr. Charles H. Shepard's early Turkish bath, that operated from 1863 until 1913. A dozen or more fine houses of the late 1820's to early 1840's, in various stages of alteration, front on Cranberry Street, especially on the north side. The main part of the Church of the Assumption, east of Hicks Street, was built in 1831, and this building was extensively remodeled and given a new façade by Bede and Burlenback, architects, in 1908. Prior to the completion of the present borough hall in 1858 the Brooklyn municipal buildings were located at the southwest intersection of Cranberry and Henry streets, later the site of the armory, and the post office was diagonally opposite. Lawyers' offices abounded in this vicinity. Walt Whitman's *Leaves of Grass* was first printed in the *building at the southwest corner of Fulton Street in 1855. As a child the poet had lived for a few years on Cranberry Street back of the site of Plymouth Church.

south side

18. 3½-storied similar to No. 15 Willow Street (corner Middagh); basement higher, making possible a more graceful curve to entrance stairs, fine wrought- and cast-iron railings encircle newel posts, contemporary fence; east flank continuous brickwork with front wall of No. 42 Willow Street; listed in 1845 city directory (No. 36) Samuel R. Daniels, merchant; full 4th story added, grille in opening to stoop

36. No. 13 Cranberry Street.

modern, part of screen wall to former open rear galleries incorporated into small enclosed addition.

66. 3-storied brick, high basement, corniced labels over windows; listed in 1840 city directory (No. 78) Rev. Samuel H. Cox; entrance lowered.

68, 70. 3-storied row houses, continuous brownstone façade, high basement, bracketed cornice, cornices on consoles over doorways, stairs Type B, contemporary fences; house on site of No. 68 listed in 1829 city directory (No. 80) E. M. M. Clarke, attorney-at-law; No. 70 listed in 1852 directory (No. 82) Conrad A. Ten Eyck, merchant.

north side

11. 3-storied, Flemish-bond brickwork on high brownstone basement; Greek Revival pilastered brownstone doorway, recessed entrance; tall windows 1st floor, 6 over 9-paned sashes, corniced labels, originally opening onto iron balcony; elaborate iron fence with anthemion designs top and bottom; house on site first listed in 1836 city directory (No. 33) Charles R. Cornell; present building perhaps built for Mott Bedell, shipmaster and later shipping merchant having a Wall Street office, who moved from No. 51 Hicks Street in 1842 and resided here until 1878; railing of entrance stairs modern, replacing late XIX cent. balustrade.

13, 15, 19. 2- or 3-storied houses, Nos. 13, 15 having continuous brick façade, No. 19 built separately, stone basement; Federal style, stonework enframing fan doorways and stone lintels above windows given panel treatment, bead-and-reel and console cornice to No. 13, wrought-iron railing to Type D stairs, pedestals probably surmounted by iron basket urns, classic lamp forms and rosettes atop iron fence posts; eight-paneled front door had leaded lunette over it and sidelights; No. 13 listed in 1829 city directory (No. 35) Richard Mortimer, and No. 15 (No. 37) John Nesmith; No. 19 listed in 1834 directory (c[orner] Willow) Dr. F. W. Ostrander (No. 39 in 1840 directory); No. 15 has 4th floor added, entrance lowered, doorway installed in garage on Obtuse Road South, Brookfield Center, Conn.; No. 19 given mansard roof, cast-iron balustrades and posts to entrance stairs, cast-iron front fence; side fence topped by anthemions, probably contemporary with house.

25. 2-storied frame with dormers; listed in 1829 city directory (No. 45) home of Mrs. Bruce; late XIX cent. bracketed cornice; renovated 1955.

51, 53. 3-storied row houses, Flemish-bond brickwork; Greek Revival, pilastered recessed doorways, entrance stairs Type D; house on site

37. Original front door to No. 15 Cranberry Street. Photograph made in 1930's, courtesy Mrs. Edward K. Hale.

of No. 51 listed in 1829 city directory (No. 65) Edward Gulliver; house on site of No. 53 listed in 1830 directory (No. 67) William Baker, sawyer, and John Moore, laborer; present buildings built about a decade later; No. 51 retains contemporary ironwork railing and fence, though pedestals flanking steps bare; entrance stairs and ironwork of No. 53 modern, frieze windows enlarged; No. 51 has original rear porch, that of No. 53 enclosed.

63. 3-storied frame house; listed in 1830 city directory (No. 77) James Brush, currier, and Benjamin J. Dobson; stuccoed, late XIX cent. bracketed cornice, railings, plate glass in windows.

65, 67. 3-storied brick duplex, Greek Revival, pilastered coupled recessed doorway capped with low-pitched pediment; houses on site listed in 1829 city directory, No. 65 (No. 79) Clement Davison, watchmaker, and No. 67 (No. 81) John B. Mayo, lawyer, and Stephen Wright, bootmaker; present building dates from about a decade later; note unusual entrance stairway with center rail and truncated stone column at foot serving as base for cast-iron post perhaps supporting a lamp originally; similar arrangement at Nos. 370, 372 State Street (outside of Heights area).

69. 3-storied frame; listed in 1829 city directory (No. 83) Richard Lawrence, carpenter, presumably its builder; walls stuccoed, ironwork modern.

Orange Street

(Supplementary illustrations nos. 77–78)

CALLED Orange Street by the Hicks brothers in the same spirit that had prompted their naming of Cranberry Street, this was the scene of a good many early-nineteenth-century frame dwellings, of which Nos. 54 and 69 are the only ones left, both of these given later mansard roofs and gingerbread details. The west end of Orange Street is dominated by the Hotel Margaret and the dormitory across from it (now under construction). Half of the south side of the block east of Willow Street is occupied by a row of bracketed houses built soon after 1850 in the style of Plymouth Church in the block beyond. Plymouth Church, erected in 1849 after a plan by J. C. Wells, is an Italianate barn-like structure that contained the largest hall in Brooklyn at the time of its construction, and was used for many public as well as for religious meetings. Henry Ward Beecher preached from its pulpit for many years, and many American notables have passed through its portals. The present Tuscan porch is twentieth century, and the parish house west of the garden court was built in 1913.

south side

22, 24, 26, 28, 30. 3-storied row houses, continuous brick façade Nos. 22–28, No. 30 being built separately, rusticated brownstone basement, sash windows made to resemble casements, bracketed cornice, plain doorways, contemporary iron railings and fences; 1851 city directory lists Henry A. Walton, Fulton Hotel NYC, occupying southeast corner of Orange and Willow streets (address given No. 49 Willow); following year lived at No. 30 (No. 48) Orange, and in 1853 his widow at No. 22 (No. 40) Orange, presumably indicating No. 30 was built first and moved into while house facing Willow was torn down and Nos. 22–28 constructed facing Orange; 1853 directory also lists No. 24 (No. 42) Edward P. Mead, merchant, No. 26 (No. 44) Willian H. Prichard, merchant, No. 28 (No. 46) Daniel Smith, Jr., merchant, and No. 30 (No. 48) George E. Brown, merchant; partition between main living rooms eliminated in favor of arch springing from wall brackets.

***52.** 3-storied brick, plain doorway, stairs Type E; listed in 1840 city directory (No. 64) Jesse W. Seaman, merchant; later doors, plate glass in windows.

***54.** 2-storied frame; listed in 1829 city directory (No. 66) William J. Hadden, dry goods merchant; late XIX cent. changes include mansard roof, doorway, windows enlarged, plate glass.

north side

69. 2-storied clapboarded frame house; listed in 1829 city directory (No. 81) widow of Garret Nostrand, also Phineas Tuttle; later XIX cent. changes include mansard roof, windows; front door, railings modern.

Pineapple Street

PINEAPPLE, the third of the four-block-long "fruit" streets named by the Hicks brothers, is mostly lined with towering, multiple dwellings, including the north sides or rear of the Towers and Saint George hotels. Several small residences are to be found in the first block off Columbia Heights, and in the block west of Henry Street across from the oldest part of the Saint George Hotel. All three examples on the north side of the street are noteworthy, No. 13 for its central-hall plan, a rarity on the Heights, and Nos. 65, 67 for their transitional Federal to Greek Revival features.

south side

12. Small 3-storied brick, stairs Type B; listed in 1850 city directory (No. 32) John B. Sardy, merchant; front doors and bay window later.

north side

13. 3-storied shingled frame house on high brick basement, 5 bays wide, due to early extension, making central stairhall plan (note lack of equal symmetry); listed in 1830 city directory (No. 33) James Hart (at end of book, under "name omitted"); 3rd story added middle of the XIX cent., front windows enlarged (original size of 1st- and 2nd-story windows may be seen rear of house); bracketed cornice late XIX cent.; fanlight to front door and stoop modern.

65, 67. 3-storied Flemish-bond brick row houses, transitional Federal to Greek Revival; attenuated Doric columns in antis flanking front door, transom over entablature, recessed enframements except for lintels over voids; stairs Type B; No. 67 listed in 1834 city directory (No. 79) Stephen Cahoon accountant; No. 65 listed in 1835 directory (No. 77) J. Sheldon; No. 65 has later plate-glass windows, glass replacing panels in door, end of XIX cent. ironwork; No. 67 late XIX cent. doorway. modern ironwork.

38. No. 13 Pineapple Street. Photograph by Edmund V. Gillon, Jr.

Clark Street

GIVEN its title after the rope walk of Captain Clark (or Clarke) that stood near Henry Street, this is the "hotel street" of Brooklyn, and consequently is the scene of much coming and going because of the social functions that are held in its two main hostelries. These are the Towers Hotel, built by Starrett and Van Vleck at Willow Street in 1928, which is primarily a residential hotel, and the other is the Saint George, famous for being the largest hotel in New York City. The Saint George was named after the eighteenth-century tavern that stood on the site of the former Colonnade Row, Columbia Heights at Cranberry Street. The earliest part of the present building is the five-storied pavilion on Pineapple Street adjacent to the tower structure on Hicks Street. It was built in 1885. The second pavilion constructed the following year faces Clark Street (ballroom entrance); and two years later the block adjacent to the east flank of the first was built on Pineapple Street. A narrow wing (no longer standing) was built on Hicks Street in 1890, and the balance of the hotel is twentieth century. The swimming pool in its basement was designed by H. Kamenka.

The early-nineteenth-century houses* opposite the Hotel Saint George have been remodeled into apartment buildings. Three Greek Revival residences in the block opposite Monroe Place still retain much of their original appearance; the ironwork of No. 97 is exceptionally fine.

south side

60. 3-storied Flemish-bond brick on high basement; listed in 1836 city directory (n[ear] Hicks) Daniel Embury, cashier L. I. Bank (No. 74 in 1838 directory); wall painted, 4th floor added, console cornice, entrance lowered.

62. 4-storied, high basement; listed in 1853 city directory (No. 76) James Forsyth, clerk; stuccoed, entrance lowered.

64. 3-storied brick, high basement; listed in 1857 city directory (No. 78) Valentine Everitt, leather (formerly at No. 80 Clark; Theodore Newman, dry goods store, lived in frame house

39. Iron fence in front of No. 97 Clark Street. Note Greek key and obelisk spikes at bottom, anthemion motif cresting.

on site in 1849); 4th story added, entrance lowered.

66. 3-storied brick house; dwelling on site listed in 1829 city directory (No. 80) William H. Case, carpenter; present structure probably that listed in 1849 directory (No. 80) Valentine Everit, leather merchant; frame attic added, entrance lowered.

north side

* **91.** 2-storied with attic, Flemish-bond brickwork; Greek Revival; listed in 1838 city directory (n[ear] Henry) Richard Everit (No. 87 in 1839 directory); entrance lowered.

95. 4-storied common-bond brickwork; Greek Revival, 1st-story stone basement treatment; listed in 1838 city directory (op[posite] Monroe) Alexander Martin, surveyor (No. 89 in 1840 directory); wall painted.

97. 4-storied common-bond brickwork, 1st of stone given rusticated basement treatment; Greek Revival, fine iron balcony 2nd-floor level, elaborate cast-iron fence with cresting of acroteria and anthemions, Greek key pattern and obelisks at bottom; listed in 1835 city directory (n[ear] Monroe Place) Charles J. Henshaw (No. 91 in 1840 directory); 1 bay added to east flank, also mansard roof; home of Paul Leicester Ford, author and historian, 1879–98.

Pierrepont Street

(Supplementary illustration no. 79)

PIERREPONT Street takes its name from Hezekiah B. Pierrepont, whose estate extended from the cliff west of Columbia Street to Moser (beyond Clinton) Street, and from Joralemon northward past Love Lane, down which the young swain used to stroll with their girl friends, the lane having been originally an Indian trail leading to a post overlooking the harbor. Since Pierrepont Street is on a direct line with South Ferry, the removal of houses at its west end affords a wide and impressive vista across the harbor. A small public park for children has been established on the site of the former Henry E. Pierrepont mansion (west side of Pierrepont Place where it joins Columbia Heights), and a sunken private garden made in the depression left by the basement of the house that stood across the street.

Although conceived much earlier Pierrepont Street was opened to the public in 1832. The oldest existing houses are Nos. 27 and 58, both built of Flemish-bond brickwork, both first listed in the 1834 city directory. The noblest residential building ever to grace Pierrepont Street was the Greek Revival duplex facing Monroe Place erected for George and P. C. Cornell before 1840, only half of which (No. 108) retains much semblance of its original form, the other half (No. 114) having been altered considerably in the Romanesque Revival idiom about 1887. Across the street stands Minard Lafever's Church of the Saviour, a delightful Gothic Revival brownstone built in 1844, the nave and side aisles of which are covered by a single roof, with skylights lighting the clerestory of the nave. Another fine contemporary Gothic Revival building is the residence at No. 36, having especially attractive ironwork in the balcony on the east flank and in the fence encircling the yard.

Outstanding houses of post Civil War vintage include the two "Romanesque" domiciles, Nos. 6 and 82, the first with its exquisite foliage carvings on the stonework of the entrance stairs, the second the design of Frank Freeman for Herman Behr, illustrated in its pristine condition in the 2 May 1891 issue of *Architecture and Building,* now enlarged into the Hotel Palm. Freeman also planned two buildings on the north corners of Clinton Street, which are the second Crescent Club building (1906) and the *Brooklyn Savings Bank (1893), the latter an especially fine example of the neo-classic style used at the Chicago Fair of 1892–93. Diagonally opposite is the red brick and terracotta home of the Long Island Historical Society designed by George B. Post and built in 1878, the front door of which is only a stone's throw away from the site of the southeast bastion of the old British fort built here during 1780–81. The Brooklyn Trust Company Building occupies the end of the block between Montague and Pierrepont across Clinton Street. This edifice in the Italian palazzo style was erected by York and Sawyer in 1915. It is now the Manufacturers Trust Company. In this small area concentric to the crossing of Pierrepont and Clinton streets is concentrated a fair number of buildings of outstanding architectural merit.

south side

22. 4-storied brownstone, Rence. Revival details including pediments on consoles over 1st-story windows, cornices on consoles over windows of upper floors; listed in 1855 city directory (No. 20) George Read, hats and caps; entrance lowered, new doorway harmonized with taste, plate glass in windows.

36. 3-storied brick on high brownstone basement, 4 bays across façade; Gothic Revival; brownstone entrance porch with hood molds over lancet arches, tracery balustrade; trefoil balustrade 2nd floor rear gallery; tracery frieze and hood molds over windows; shallow balcony of delicate cast-iron work, covered by dipping roof, on main floor of Hicks Street side; fine contemporary cast-iron fence encloses yard; listed in 1845 city directory (c[orner] Hicks) George Hastings, merchant (No. 32 in 1849 directory); plate glass in windows; front steps of porch removed, section of former railing inserted between posts, which accounts for quatrefoil leaning at rakish angle; narrow addition on west flank.

48. 3-storied brick; listed in 1842 city directory (No. 42) Henry Manning, merchant; story added, entrance lowered.

50. 3-storied brick; listed in 1842 city directory (No. 44) Mrs. Sarah Richards; late XIX cent. mansard roof, hood molds over windows, Romanesque Revival doorway, stone and iron rails, plate glass.

56. 3-storied, Flemish-bond brickwork; listed in 1840 city directory (No. 48) George A. Talbot, merchant; late XIX cent. mansard roof, Eastlake details, iron balustrade and iron fence, colored glass in inner doors, plate glass in windows.

58. 3-storied Flemish-bond brickwork on high stone basement; listed in 1834 city directory (No. 50) E. N. Gregory, merchant; mansard roof added, late XIX cent. doorway, hood molds, entrance stairs and ironwork.

60. 3-storied brick on high basement; Greek Revival, doorway with "Greek ears," corniced labels over windows; listed in 1849 city directory (No. 52) Peter Balen, fruit merchant; later mansard roof, stone and iron entrance stairway, plate-glass windows.

76, 80. 3½-storied duplex, continuous brick façade, high basement, corniced labels over windows, windows of three lights over doorways; No. 76 listed in 1844 city directory (No. 62) Lowell Holbrook, merchant; No. 80 in 1845 directory (No. 64) T. S. Nelson; No. 76 has late XIX cent. bay window over entrance porch, balustrades, console cornices over windows, plate glass, iron fence; No. 80 later mansard roof, entrance lowered, plate glass, modern fence.

86. 3-storied brick; listed in 1844 city directory (No. 68 c[orner] Henry) Lewis Tappan, mercantile agent; story added, walls stuccoed, plate glass.

98, 100, 102. 4-storied row houses, continuous brownstone façade, each 2 bays wide, console cornice, hoods over windows, balcony at 2nd-floor level; No. 100 listed in 1857 city directory (No. 76) Henry B. Cromwell, shipping merchant; Nos. 98 and 102 listed in 1860 directory, (No. 74) A. G. Robertson, broker, and (No. 78) Alfred N. Hoyt; entrances lowered, iron fences modern.

104. 4-storied brownstone, console cornice, hoods with consoles or brackets over doorway and windows, elaborately carved 1st and 2nd stories; listed in 1858 city directory (No. 80) Thomas Clark, fancy store; ironwork later.

108. 3-storied, common-bond brick façade (originally covered with sanded paint or stucco), quoins at west corners of 2 pavilions, each 2 bays wide, high stone basement; house was half of duplex that included No. 114; Greek Revival, pedimented doorway with acroteria, corniced labels over windows, entrance stairs originally Type E, gable pediment spanned 4-bayed center pavilion, round frieze windows to 3rd story, cupola on center of roof, balcony along 1st-floor level, raised terrace adjacent to sidewalk, plan similar to that of No. 70 willow with circular open-newel staircase; listed in 1840 city directory (op[posite] Monroe) P. C. Cornell; 3rd story heightened, bracketed cornice; remodeled 1907 for George Hunt Prentiss, including recessed fan "colonial" door, bay window next entrance, plate glass, railings and blocks flanking entrance steps removed, ironwork replaced, terrace eliminated.

114. Originally balance of duplex with No. 108; listed in 1840 city directory (op[posite] Monroe) George Cornell (indicated in house directory on east side of P. C. Cornell); remodeled for Alfred C. Barnes, publisher, who took up residence here *ca.* 1887; brownstone, brick, and terracotta façade, Romanesque Revival style with turret, gable, rounded bays, reliefs, ironwork; some original mantels (black marble) and woodwork retained, open-newel circular staircase removed for one of straight flights, hall woodwork of later period; purchased 1912 by Brooklyn Women's Club for headquarters, alterations by Katherine Budd, architect; new assembly rooms made, entrance lowered.

116. 3-storied brick, high basement; Greek Revival, pilastered doorway, stairs Type B, corniced labels over windows; listed in 1844 city directory (n[ear] Clinton) Thomas Carpenter (No. 88 in 1847 directory); later door, plate glass.

118. 3-storied brownstone, console cornice, arched doorway; listed in 1858 city directory (No. 90) Hosea Webster, pres. savings bank; stuccoed, including railing and fence.

120. 4-storied; listed in 1858 city directory (No. 92) John Meyher, merchant; stuccoed, entrance lowered, ironwork modern.

122, 124, 126. 3-storied brownstone row houses, console cornices, arched doorways, balustraded stairways; 1860 city directory lists No. 122 (No. 94) James B. and William H. Carter, merchants, and No. 126 (No. 98) John H. Funk, builder; No. 124 listed in 1861 directory (No. 96) Henry Sheldon, grocer; balustrades of Nos. 122, 124 filled in with stucco; entrance lowered of No. 126, stuccoed.

north side

9, 15. 4-storied row houses, continuous brownstone façade, Rence. Revival, console cornices, enframed segmented arched windows; listed in 1856 city directory (No. 5) Stephen Linington, grocer, and (No. 7) Henry G. Reeve, grocer, and John Topping, merchant; doorways al-

40. Façade of Nos. 108–14 Pierrepont Street about a century ago, before east half was remodeld, circa *1887. Courtesy Mrs. Dudley Campbell.*

tered, bay windows 2nd floor, later ironwork; railings modern.

19. 5-storied; listed in 1854 city directory (No. 11 n[ear] Willow) Charles H. Baxter, merchant (No. 9 in 1855 directory); stripped of details, stuccoed, entrance lowered, plate glass in windows.

21, 23, 25. 5-storied brownstones, each 2 bays wide, treated as single composition with pediment over center house, Rence. Revival, frieze and cornice over enframement of windows on 2nd, 3rd, and 4th stories, 1st story given rusticated basement treatment, balcony at 2nd-floor level; Nos. 23, 25 listed in 1856 city directory, (No. 13) Robert Spear, and (No. 15) Victor Fleury, importer; No. 21 in 1859 directory

(No. 11) Robert Ellis, hardware; balustrade of balcony removed, bay windows added; fire escape on No. 25, changes to east flank. No. 21 home of Judge Willard Bartlett (died 1925), drama critic and writer of editorials on legal topics for *New York Sun,* Prof. Medical Jurisprudence at Long Island College Hospital, 1892–1916.

27. 3-storied brick, front laid Flemish bond; one of earliest Greek Revival buildings on Heights; listed in 1834 city directory (c[orner] Willow) Henry Thomas, hardware merchant; home of Joseph Sands beginning 1836 (former residence No. 122 Willow Street); fine contemporary side fence with anthemion cresting and Greek key design; front fence and mansard roof late XIX cent.; entrance lowered, showing remains of channeled Doric columns to original doorway; frieze over parlor doorways from design by Minard Lafever; interior remodeled 1959.

31. 3-storied brick, probably orginally Greek Revival; listed in 1836 city directory (n[ear] Willow) Edward Carington, indicated to be adjacent to Joseph Sands in the street directory published in the 1840 Brooklyn city directory; changes include mansard roof, superimposed bay windows, Rence. Revival details over 1st-floor windows, late XIX cent. ironwork, modern repairs to doorway.

71. 3-storied, Flemish-bond brickwork, 1st-story basement treatment of stone; Greek Revival, small distyle Doric entrance portico (now removed), fine contemporary cast-iron fence with anthemion motif; west half of duplex; listed in 1840 city directory (n[ear] Henry) William H. Phillips, agent (Moses Phillips shown occupying east side in 1840 house guide, M. Phillips listed No. 53 in 1845 directory; W. H. Phillips last listed on Pierrepont Street in 1842 directory); two stories added, later doors, plate glass.

79, 81. 3-storied duplex; No. 79 listed in 1845 city directory (No. 55) Cyrus P. Smith, lawyer (had been No. 51 in 1843 and 1844 directories); No. 81 in 1855 directory (No. 57) Thomas Nelson, merchant (listed No. 61 in 1854 directory); 4th floor added, bracketed cornice; stuccoed.

123, 125. 3-storied brick row houses, façade brickwork not continuous, corniced labels over windows; No. 123 listed in 1849 city directory (n[ear] Clinton) E. Lyman (No. 93, E. H. R. Lyman, importer, in 1850 directory); No. 125 in 1850 directory (No. 95) Lucius Hopkins, merchant; No. 125 has 4th story added; both entrances lowered, plate glass; untenanted for several years.

41. Montague Street before 1904. Garden of former John T. Martin house, center. House on right is rear of No. 36 Pierrepont Street, corner of Hicks Street. Courtesy Long Island Historical Society.

Montague Street

WHATEVER century-old buildings still exist along Montague Street have been spoiled by modern display windows and shop fronts defacing the lower parts, so that no specific examples here will be analyzed, yet the street itself has an interesting history, and deserves some comment.

On the 1831 map of the Hezekiah B. Pierrepont property the street is shown extending only between Hicks and Clinton streets, and is labeled Constable Street, after Mrs. Pierrepont's family. The eighteenth-century Pierrepont mansion, Four Chimneys, straddled the site of what became the continuation of Constable, midway between Hicks and what was then Columbia Street. The name of Constable Street was changed by Henry Evelyn Pierrepont in honor of Lady Mary Wortley Montague, born Pierrepont, the English author. A short street, entitled Evelyn, between Fulton and Moser (no longer existing) was absorbed into Montague Street, which acquired definitive form around 1850. At that time it descended to the harbor, connecting with the Wall Street Ferry. During the mid 1850's Minard Lafever built the picturesque stone arch across the incline a little to the west of Pierrepont Place and Montague Terrace, which, after 1870, were made accessible to one another also by an iron passerelle called the "Penny Bridge," taken down in 1946. The descent to the ferry started about on a line with No. 63 Montague Street.

No. 75 is the Heights Casino, designed by William Alciphron Baring, Jr., opened during October, 1905. The Hotel Bossert, built by Frank Helmle in 1909, at the southeast intersection of Hicks Street, occupies the site of the Pierrepont House, a leading mid-nineteenth-century hostelry. Several Romanesque Revival hotels and apartment houses are in the block opposite the Bossert. The south side of Montague Street between Henry and Clinton is made up of uniform four-storied brownstones, most of which have their basement and main stories converted into business places. On the southwest corner of Clinton Street stands the tall, yellow-brick-and-stone Franklin Trust Company Building, erected in 1891 after a "Romanesque" design by George L. Morse. Across from it is Lafever's Church of the Holy Trinity (1844–47) facing Clinton Street. Beginning on the northeast corner is a row of distinguished banking houses, the first and handsomest being that of the Brooklyn Trust Company (now Manufacturers Trust Company), a beautifully detailed palazzo design by York and Sawyer erected in 1915. Next to it is the small classic portico of the People's Trust Company (now First National City Bank) built by Mowbray and Uffinger in 1904. The Chase Manhattan Bank adjoining is a tall building with *Arts Décoratif* ornaments, the work of

Corbett, Harrison, and MacMurray, 1929. Also in this block was the former Brooklyn Mercantile Library, later a branch of the Brooklyn Public Library and a Business Library. It was designed by Peter B. Wight in the polychromed Venetian Gothic or Ruskinian manner, Built during 1867–69, demolition of the structure was begun in March, 1960.

Remsen Street

(Supplementary illustration no. 80)

REMSEN Street was opened in 1825 by Henry Remsen, who lived in the area that became Grace Court. On the 1831 map of the Pierrepont property it is shown running from Columbia to Clinton streets. The modern turnaround at the west end of Remsen Street, which connects with the south extremity of the Esplanade, affords one of the nicest views across the water surrounding Manhattan Island that is to be had from the Heights. Three of its four tree-lined blocks shade mid- to late-nineteenth-century houses and occasional apartment buildings of later date. The outstanding edifice on Remsen Street is Richard Upjohn's Church of the Pilgrims, facing Henry Street. At Clinton stands the First Church of Brooklyn, New York Presbytery (old school), built 1850–53, now called the Spencer Memorial Church. Except for the Renaissance Revival façade of the earlier part of the Brooklyn Union Gas Company, the commercial buildings in the last block approaching Court Street do not have the interest of those on Montague Street near Borough Hall.

south side

10. 4-storied; listed in 1844 city directory (No. 4) Henry Stevens, merchant; later bracketed cornice, hoods over windows, entrance lowered, doorway "colonial," plate glass.

12. 4-storied; listed in 1844 city directory (No. 6) E. T. H. Gibson; remodeled in 1956, refaced with brick, void pattern changed, entrance lowered.

14. 3-storied brick, Greek Revival, pilastered doorway; listed in 1845 city directory (No. 8) George Townsend; late XIX cent. mansard roof, door and ironwork, plate glass.

16, 18. 3-storied row houses, continuous brick façade, high basement, late Greek Revival, scrolled pediments on brackets over doorways, stairs Type B; listed in 1852 city directory (No. 10) Thomas Baylis, builder, and (No. 12) Samuel Barber, merchant; bracketed cornice, plate glass, modern railings.

20. 3-storied brick, similar to Nos. 16, 18, contemporary railing and fence; listed in 1856 city directory (No. 14) David Buffum, dry goods.

22. 3-storied brownstone, bracketed cornice, hoods on brackets over windows, pediment on brackets over doorway, stairs Type B; listed in 1853 city directory (No. 16) G. L. Willard, commission merchant; 4th floor added (brick).

28. 3-storied; house on site listed in 1841 city directory (Remsen Columbia) John Prentice, furrier (Remsen n[ear] Columbia in 1842 directory, No. 22 in 1845 directory); brownstone front with Rence. Revival details perhaps added contemporaneous with building of adjoining house, No. 30; some renovation, cement wall in front, plate glass in windows.

30. 3-storied brownstone, similar to No. 28; listed in 1853 directory (No. 24) Crowell Hadden, merchant; bay window 2nd floor; entrance lowered.

34, 36. 3-storied, continuous brownstone façade; Rence. Revival and other details; 1846 city directory lists house on site of No. 34 (No. 28) Frederick W. Boell; No. 36 in 1849 directory (No. 30) George Beulen, clerk; listed in 1853 directory as respective homes of Edward Lyman and Josiah O. Low; mansard roofs probably later.

42, 44. 3-storied, continuous brick façade; listed in 1844 city directory (No. 32) Brazilla Ransom, and (No. 34) Augustus R. Moore, merchant; stripped of details, entrances lowered, plate glass in windows, mansard roofs.

46. 3-storied brick; listed in 1846 city directory (No. 36) A. C. Richards, merchant; later mansard roof, projecting entrance bay with door at basement level; stuccoed front; interesting rear wing added during 1920's (visible from Grace Court) of brick, terracotta, and brownstone, having parapet gable with sun dial, gargoyles, and clustered bay windows containing stained glass; room on third level has high-pitched beamed ceiling, carved brackets at springing of beams, clerestory lighting, oak paneling in XVII cent. style including figures and architectural motifs, rustic fireplace in southwest corner, parquetry floor.

48. 3-storied brick; listed in 1844 city directory (No. 38) William H.

Priest, auctioneer; Rence. Revival moldings around windows capped by frieze and cornice, mansard roof, bay window 2nd floor over pedimented console doorway, balustrade fence. plate glass.

50. 3-storied brick; listed in 1844 city directory (No. 40) John Slade; later additional story, console pediment over doorway, door "colonial," wall stuccoed, plate glass, ironwork.

52, 54, 58. 3-storied row houses, continuous brick façade, high basement; Greek Revival, pilastered doorways, stairs Type B; listed in 1844 city directory (No. 42) Alpheus Forbes, (No. 44) F. A. Lee, merchant, and (No. 46) Samuel Morgan, merchant; No. 52 has later bracketed cornice, studio window 1st story, modern ironwork; No. 58 has mansard roof, pediment on consoles over doorway and windows, modern ironwork.

82. 3-storied, Flemish-bond brickwork, high basement, 4 bays wide; listed in 1843 city directory (No. 62) William S. Packer, merchant (William Satterlee Packer, benefactor of Packer Collegiate Institute, lived here until his villa was completed overlooking the harbor at the end of Grace Court in 1850); later console cornice, modern "Tudor" openings 1st story, plate glass in upper windows.

84. 3-storied, Flemish-bond brickwork, high basement, 4 bays wide; listed in 1840 city directory (No. 64) Oliver H. Gordon, merchant; later mansard roof, quoins, window enframements with hood cornices or pediments (1st floor), plate glass, entrance lowered.

88. 4-storied brick on high stone basement, Rence. Revival details including carved brownstone console cornices over doorway and windows, entrance stairs Type B; building on site listed in 1838 city directory (n[ear] Henry N. D. C. Moller, merchant (No. 66 in 1840 directory), this house perhaps incorporated in present structure (Greek Revival woodwork in 2nd-story chambers), though outer visible style belongs to post Civil War period; rear addition and parlors main floor remodeled in "colonial" or "Adam" fashion, 1906.

92. 2-storied, Flemish-bond brickwork, high basement; apparently listed in 1835 city directory (n[ear] Henry) Edward Whitehouse (No. 68 in 1837 directory, No. 70 in 1846 directory); 3rd story and mansard roof added, plate glass in windows; entrance lowered, basement and 1st-story wall stuccoed.

94. 2-storied, Flemish-bond brickwork, high basement; late Federal (transitional) style, doorway with Ionic columns, leaded glass, stone enframement, stone lintels above windows; rococo-gothic cage posts on pedestals flanking entrance steps; listed in 1838 city directory (n[ear] Henry) Charles H. Sands, merchant (name given Christian H. Sands, indicated adjacent to E. Whitehouse

42. Remsen Street looking westward, showing tower of the Church of the Pilgrims, 1860's. From Henry R. Stiles, History...of the County of Kings and the City of Brooklyn, *New York, 1884, Vol. I.*

at No. 68 in 1840 house guide; listed No. 72 in 1844 directory); 3rd story has been added.

96. 3-storied Flemish-bond brickwork, high basement; listed in 1835 city directory (n[ear] Henry) John Skillman (indicated adjacent to Samuel Boyd, Jr., corner of Henry, in 1840 house guide); late XIX cent. bracketed cornice, moldings around windows, doorway, balustrade and posts.

110. 3-storied; listed in 1855 city directory (No. 76) Day O. Kellogg, iron; 4th story added, stuccoed, entrance lowered.

114. 4-storied brownstone, Rence. Revival, console cornice, elaborately carved friezes and consoles supporting cornices over 1st-, 2nd-, and 3rd-story openings, balustrades to entrance stairs; house indicated on 1860 map (No. 78) but number could not be found in city directories up to 1863.

116. 4-storied brownstone, Rence. Revival, frieze and cornice over enframed windows; listed in 1858 city directory (No. 80) Philo B. Gilbert, silverware; entrance lowered.

118. 4-storied, console cornice; listed in 1856 city directory (No. 82) John Dalton, blacksmith; stuccoed, entrance lowered.

128. 3-storied brownstone, Rence. Revival, console cornice, frieze and cornice over enframed windows, Corinthian pilasters to doorway, balcony at 1st-floor level; listed in 1856 city directory (No. 90) Jane Thompson (colored) widow of John; iron railings and fence modern.

138, 140. 3-storied brownstones, Rence. Revival, console cornice, hoods or pediments on consoles over windows and doors, elaborate carving; No. 138 listed in 1856 city directory (No. 96) Frederic Fuller, confectioner; No. 140 in 1858 directory (No. 98) S. A. Baum, widow; entrances lowered; basement and 1st story of No. 140 commercial; No. 138 has 4th story added.

north side

77. 3-storied brownstone, segmented arched windows, pediment on consoles over entrance; listed in 1857 city directory (No. 61) William M. Vail, dry goods; 4th story added (brick) 1959.

79, 81, 83, 85. 3-storied duplexes, continuous brick façade, corniced labels over windows, plain recessed doorways, scrolled ironwork on stone-wall sections flanking entrance stairs, contemporary fences; indicated as new buildings in 1840 house guide; No. 81 listed in 1841 city directory (n[ear] Henry) John Sneden, distiller (No. 65 in 1844 directory); No. 85 in 1843 directory (n[ear] Henry) Hamilton Blake, merchant

43. No. 123 Remsen Street. Photograph by Edmund V. Gillon, Jr.

(No. 69 in 1844 directory); Nos. 79, 83 in 1844 directory (No. 63) Joseph A. Perry, merchant, and (No. 67 n[ear] Henry) Joshua Steele, merchant; later doorways; Nos. 79, 81, 85 have bracketed cornices, plate glass; No. 85 has bay window over entrance.

89, 91, 93. 3-storied row houses, continuous brick façade; indicated new buildings in 1840 house guide; No. 91 listed in 1842 city directory (n[ear] Henry) Isaac H. Bassett (No. 75 in 1844 directory); No. 89 in 1843 directory (n[ear] Henry) Gold S. Silliman (No. 73 in 1844 directory); and No. 93 in 1844 directory (No. 77 c[orner] Henry) W. K. Brown, physician; No. 89 has console cornice, hoods and other stonework around door and windows, modern railing; No. 91 has mansard roof, stone hoods with Eastlake details, modern railings and fence; No. 93 has mansard roof, entrance lowered, stone hoods over windows, late XIX cent. iron fence; all have plate-glass windows.

113. 3-storied brownstone, mansard roof, cornices over windows, pediment on consoles over doorway; listed in 1855 city directory (No. 83) Oliver N. Bostwick, merchant; stairs and wall in front later.

115. 3-storied; listed in 1860 city directory (No. 83) P. C. Adams, merchant (had been No. 85 on 1855 map, changed to No. 83 on 1860 map); stuccoed.

117. 3-storied brownstone, console cornice, segmented arched windows, carving over arch of entrance; listed in 1856 city directory (No. 85) Henry Nesmith, shipping (No. 117 in 1871 directory); stuccoed walls to stair railings replace balustrades; now Brooklyn Engineers' Club.

123. 3-storied plus mansard roof, brick and stone, 3-part composition, Corinthian columns to shallow entrance porch, balustrades and impressive stone newel posts; listed in 1856 city directory (No. 87) Charles Condon, iron; now headquarters of Brooklyn Bar Association.

125. 3-storied brownstone, console cornice, cornice hoods on consoles over 1st-story openings; listed in 1857 city directory (No. 89) Elmira Gardner; ironwork later.

127. 3-storied; listed in 1857 city directory (No. 91) D. H. Gould, saloon; 4th story added, entrance lowered, stuccoed.

131. 3-storied brownstone, 3-part composition, elaborate console cornice, Corinthian columns in antis at entrance; listed in 1858 city directory (No. 95) Terrence McDonald, hemp; doorway lowered, stuccoed; now the Brooklyn Club.

44. No. 67 Joralemon Street looking westward.

Grace Court

(Supplementary illustrations nos. 81 and 82)

GRACE Court takes its name from Grace P. E. Church, a Gothic Revival brownstone edifice built in 1847 after a design by Richard Upjohn on the south corner of Hicks Street at the present entrance to Grace Court, with a parish house of similar style constructed behind in 1931.

During the latter half of the nineteenth century two large mansions stood on the bluff facing the harbor in this area, on a line with the contemporary Henry E. Pierrepont and the Alexander M. White and A. A. Low houses on Pierrepont Place. One of the Grace Court mansions was the Italianate villa built for William Satterlee Packer in 1850, which was located about on the site of the entrance court of the big apartment building now designated No. 2, erected after the Packer home was demolished in 1916. The other one was the 3-storied and attic, frame John H. Prentice mansion, which was located on the site of No. 19 Grace Court.

Three city residences were built on the north side of the street prior to a century ago, the first one (No. 27) for the Rev. Francis Vinton, rector of Grace Church. To the east of these houses is the row of deep back yards to residences on Remsen Street, which have tall iron fences on stone copings around their lush planting, forming the unique feature of the street. An alignment of late-nineteenth-century brownstones intervenes Grace Church Parish House and the massive modern apartment building on the south side of Grace Court.

The continuation of Grace Court across Hicks Street is called Grace Court Alley, which is equally as attractive and unusual as its counterpart because of its assortment of stables and carriage-houses converted into dwellings.

north side

27. 3-storied, Rence. Revival, 1st story given basement treatment with rusticated stonework, 2 bays wide, quoins at corners; listed in 1855 city directory (Grace Court) Francis Vinton, Rev. (rector of Grace Church, No. 3 in 1856 directory, No. 5 in 1857 directory); 2 stories added, the top one an enclosed loggia, ironwork at entrance modern.

29. 3-storied brownstone, Rence. Revival, console cornice, hoods over enframements around openings; listed in 1856 city directory (No. 5) John Porg; recessed balcony cut through cornice, later railings, plate glass.

31. 3-storied, originally probably mate to No. 29; listed in 1857 city directory (No. 9) Louis Ludovici, hidebroker; stuccoed, plate glass in windows.

Joralemon Street

(Supplementary illustrations nos. 83 and 84)

ONCE THE south boundary of the Remsen farm, connecting the distillery at its foot with the village located around present-day Borough Hall, Joralemon Street cuts across at an angle not quite parallel nor perpendicular to neighboring streets. A ferry to New York was established at the lower end in 1693, but its function was later taken over by those at Fulton Street, Montague Street, and Atlantic Avenue. Named after Teunis Joralemon, who acquired the Livingston property in 1803, the old road became known as Joralemon's Lane after 1805.

A few houses were built on the north side between Henry and Clinton streets during the 1830's, such as Nos. 135 and 139. The lane became a street in 1842, and many more houses sprang up almost overnight, especially along the stretch west of Hicks Street. The slope of the street down to the river creates a picturesque setting for the little three-storied Greek Revival row dwellings, most of which retain their original pilastered doorways and iron railings. At the southwest corner of Columbia Place stand the Riverside Houses, model tenements built by Alfred T. White in 1889–90. Both brick and brownstone residences are to be found along Joralemon Street after it levels off east of

45. Entrance to No. 135 Joralemon Street.

Hicks Street. Apartment buildings alternate with the early houses as one nears Clinton Street, and on the southwest corner rises the large Medical Arts and Insurance Company Buildings. Eastward are the pavilions of Packer Collegiate Institute, the earliest of which was built in the Gothic Revival style after designs by Minard Lafever in 1854. The balance of this block and that across from the institute are given over to commercial enterprises, with tall office buildings on Court Street.

south side

40, 42, 44. 3-storied row houses, each 2 bays wide, continuous brick façade, Nos. 42, 44 on same level, No. 40 lower, triple window and plain doorway 1st story, had shallow porches; listed in 1846 city directory, No. 40 (No. 21) Albert Gates, No. 42 (No. 23) Paul Weizel, prof. of music, and No. 44 (No. 25) George Bent, merchant; modern doors, changes in windows, especially No. 44 having stanchions removed from triple window.

56. 3-storied, similar to No. 37 group, front brick wall continuous with north flank of No. 1 Willow Place; listed in 1849 city directory (No. 41) Howard Cady, lawyer.

58, 60. 3-storied row houses, similar to No. 37 group, continuous brick façade though houses are on different levels; listed in 1847 city directory (No. 43) Byron Wilkinson, and (No. 45) Daniel Stamant, importer of wine; No. 58 serves as IRT subway vent, given steel shutters; entrance stairs and railing altered.

84, 86. 3-storied row houses, continuous brick façade, plain recessed doorways, stairs Type B (No. 84 only); listed in 1847 city directory (No. 61) Lathrop Stafford, merchant, and Robert Ayres, clerk, and (No. 63) Rev. N. W. White and A. D. Wheelock, shoe dealer; No. 86 has later stairs.

88. 3-storied brick house, similar to Nos. 84, 86; listed in 1849 city directory (No. 65) Edward H. Arnold, merchant; Eastlake details later.

90. 3-storied brick, scrolled pediment on consoles over entrance; listed in 1855 city directory (No. 67) Agnes McClume, widow of Thomas; railings later.

94. 3-storied brick, 5 bays wide, central-hall plan; listed in 1854 city directory (No. 69) John P. Atkinson, merchant; walls resurfaced with brick because of subway vibrations, plate glass in windows, Tuscan di-style portico at entrance, ironwork modern, now YWCA.

96, 98. 3-storied row houses, continuous brick façade, plain recessed entrances, stairs Type B; No. 96 listed in 1846 city directory (n[ear] Henry) H. F. Lombard (No. 71 n[ear] Henry in 1851 directory); No. 98 in 1851 directory (No. 73) Harriet Phillips, widow of Moses, and Misses Phillips Young Ladies' School; No. 96 has bay window on 2nd-story front, entrance stairs and railings modern.

108. 4-storied brick, contemporary fence; listed in 1849 city directory (Henry n[ear] Joralemon) Daniel E. Kissam, physician (No. 154 Henry n[ear] Joralemon in 1850 directory); modern door.

118. 3-storied brick, 2-part composition, entrance stairs Type B; listed in 1848 city directory (No. 75) George W. Baxter, merchant; bracketed cornice, later door, plate glass.

120, 122, 124, 126. 3-storied row houses, continuous brick façade, cornices over windows, pediments over plain doorways, stairs Type B, contemporary fences; No. 122 listed in 1847 city directory (n[ear] Henry) Charles Bridges, bookkeper (No. 79 in 1848 directory); others listed in 1848 directory, (No. 77) William Himrod, merchant, (No. 81) Benjamin Haskell, and (No. 83) J. W. Jones, commission merchant; No. 122 has entrance lowered, modern metal casement windows 1st story.

134. 4-storied brick and stone, Rence. Revival, cornices over enframed windows, iron balustrades; listed in 1858 city directory (No. 91) J. C. Herman Trost, glassware.

136, 138. 4-storied row houses, continuous brownstone façade, Rence. Revival, console cornice, frieze and cornices over openings; No. 138 listed in 1855 city directory (No. 27 [*sic*] Michael Chauncey, builder (No. 95 in 1856 and 1857 directories); No. 136 in 1856 directory (No. 93) Darius Geer, importer; No. 136 has studio 4th floor; entrance to No. 138 lowered.

140. 3-storied brownstone, Rence. Revival, console cornice, frieze and cornices over windows, cornice on consoles over arched doorway, iron balustrades; listed in 1855 city directory (No. 97) David and Daniel Chauncey, builders (No. 95 in 1856 directory, No. 97 in 1857 directory).

north side

29, 31, 35. 3-storied row houses, brick, Nos. 29, 31 have continuous façade; plain recessed doorways, stairs Type E; Nos. 29, 31 listed in 1845 city directory (No. 6) R. A. Lyons, and (No. 8) Agnes Sage, widow, and L. Sage, clerk; No. 35 in 1846 directory (No. 12) Charles A. Strong; Nos. 29, 35 have parapets added, plate glass in windows.

37, 39, 41, 43, 45, 47, 49, 51, 53, 55, 57, 59, 61, 63, 65, 67, 69, 71, 73, 75, (also 260 Hicks). 3-storied row houses built on incline, each pair raised about 30 inches above level of pair to the west; continuous brick façades in groups of from two to four: 37–39–41, 43–45–47–49, 51–53, 55–57–59, 61–63–65, 67–69 (Nos. 71, 73, 75, and 260 Hicks altered); Greek Revival, pilastered recessed doorways, entrance stairs Type F (steps without nosings); 1844 city directory lists No. 63 (n[ear] Hicks) William M. Peck (No. 42 in 1845 directory), No. 75 (n[ear] Hicks) J. S. Hyde (James Hyde, No. 54 in 1845 directory); 1845 directory lists No. 37 (No. 14) James Rowan, lumber merchant, No. 41 (No. 18) Paul Weizel, prof. of music, No. 43 (No. 20) James Chadbourne, No. 45 (No. 22) Isaac L. Condit, merchant, No. 49 (No. 26) Silas Davenport, merchant; No. 51 (No. 28) William R. Starkwater, No. 53 (No. 30) Lewis F. Mack, broker, No. 61 (No. 40) Francis Sterling, No. 69 (No. 48) B. F. Browning, merchant, No. 73 (No. 52) Phillip H. Wentworth; 1846 directory lists No. 39 (No. 16) Gabriel Franchere, fur dealer, No. 47 (No. 24) Henry Haydock, No. 65 (No. 44) Bernardus Everson, merchant, No. 67 (No. 46) E. W. Coleman, No. 71 (No. 50) Jeremiah P. Robinson; 1848 directory lists No. 55 (No. 32) Michael Van Buren, merchant (this house designated No. 34 on 1855 map, adjacent to Nos. 30, 36), No. 57 (No. 36) Francis Vincent, merchant, and No. 59 (No. 38) Joseph Grice, commission merchant (see also No. 260 Hicks Street); later changes include enlargement of 3rd-story windows of Nos. 37, 45, 49, 55, 59, 63, 65, 69, wall heightened into parapet of Nos. 45, 53, 55, 57, entrances lowered of Nos. 53, 57, 59; minor changes to doors, many with plate glass in windows; Nos. 71, 73, 75 remodeled early XX cent., given new brick facing and details including metal bracketed cornice.

135. 2½-storied clapboarded frame house with curb roof, dormers, basement of Flemish-bond brickwork, Federal style house similar to No. 24 Middagh Street (plan reversed), representative of a number of houses of this type that stood in this block on Joralemon Street; lot shown as belonging to Allen Lippincott on 1831 map of Isaac T. Ludlam, village surveyor; house listed in city directory of 1833 (No. 90 Jarolemon [*sic*] Dr. Haslett (Dr. John Haslett, USN, No. 88 in 1834 directory; John Haslet, Surgeon, USN, No. 90 in 1840 directory); cast-iron porch added after mid XIX cent. and 1st-floor windows elongated; glass replaces 4 wood panels in front door; rear porch with slender colonnettes between narrow closet flankers has had part of floor removed to light new picture window in basement kitchen.

137. 3-storied brick, high stone base-

46. Detail of No. 57 Livingston Street.

ment; listed in 1847 city directory (No. 92) Martha Boyd, widow (No. 94 in 1843–46 directories); modern brick facing and other changes.

139. 3-storied brick, high stone basement; Federal style, exquisitely carved cornucopias in panels of stone lintels over windows and original doorway; listed in 1830 city directory (No. 94) A. T. Goodrich, bookseller; house indicated on 1831 Ludlam map under same name, occupying center of 3 lots; modern additional story, entrance lowered.

149. 3-storied, Flemish-bond brickwork, high basement; listed in 1829 city directory (No. 102) John Lawrence, 1st Marshall (identified as sheriff in 1834 directory); house indicated on 1831 Ludlam map; details spoiled, late XIX cent. mansard roof added, railing modern.

Livingston Street

LIVINGSTON Street points in the direction of the former Philip Livingston residence (*ca.* 1764) that stood on the east side of Hicks Street, near Joralemon. The two blocks that enter the Heights area are considerably narrower than the balance of the street extending eastward. Houses began to be built on Livingston Street during the early 1840's, and one finds several dwellings of the Revival periods on the south side between Clinton and Court streets, including an unusual little Gothic Revival example with lace-like ironwork (No. 52). Across Livingston Street in this block are the flank of Saint Anne's P. E. Church (1867–69) at the corner of Clinton Street, the back of Packer Collegiate Institute facing Joralemon, and, to the side of the institute lot, one very fine Greek Revival residence retaining its contemporary iron balcony and fence (No. 57).

south side

42, 44, 46, 48. 3-storied brick, corniced labels over windows; 1847 city directory lists No. 44 (No. 22) Henry Van Duyne, and No. 46 (No. 24) Thomas Stratton, mason; 1848 directory lists No. 42 (No. 20) George Ribley, merchant, and No. 48 (No. 26) Thomas W. Blachford, merchant; later bracketed cornices; Nos. 46, 48 console doorways; No. 46

late XIX cent. railing; No. 48 modern stairs; No. 42, 44 entrances lowered, No. 44 doorway "colonial"; plate glass and other changes to windows.

50. 3-storied brick; listed in 1846 city directory (No. 30) Charles Congdon, merchant (No. 28 in 1847 directory); later mansard roof, console doorway, plate glass; front wall covered with synthetic yellow brick.

52. 2-storied brick; listed in 1846 city directory (No. 32 n[ear] Court) Matilda Brown, widow (No. 30 n[ear] Court in 1847 directory); remodeled in romantic style probably after building of Packer Collegiate Institute across street in 1854; Gothic Revival details include dripmolds over windows and recessed front door, shallow cast-iron tracery porch and matching fence, newel posts capped with pinnacles; parlor made octagonal with corner niches, ribs on flat ceiling radiating from centerpiece give effect of low dome, projecting doorway from stairhall balances chimney breast and adds spaciousness to narrow passage; later changes include addition of 3rd story, front wall stuccoed, modern metal casement windows.

54, 56. 3-storied, continuous brick façade on high brownstone basement; No. 54 3 bays wide, stripped of details; No. 56 4 bays wide, Greek Revival, pediment over recessed doorway with "Greek ears" to enframement, shallow intaglio carvings above basement windows and on doorway, plan similar to that of No. 90 State, No. 70 Willow and Nos. 108–114 Pierrepont; 1846 city directory lists No. 54 (No. 34) M. W. Butt (listed as No. 32 in 1847 directory), and No. 56 (No. 36 n[ear] Court) Palmer Townsend (No. 34 in 1847 directory); No. 54 has 4th story added, entrance lowered; No. 56 has later doors, stairs and railings; both have plate glass.

62. 3-storied brick; listed in 1845 city directory (n[ear] Court) Stanford Cobb, merchant (No. 38 in 1846 directory, No. 36 in 1847 directory); stripped of details, entrance lowered, plate glass.

north side

57. 3-storied brick on high basement, Greek Revival, recessed doorway enframed with brownstone pilasters and entablature, entrance steps Type B; contemporary ironwork includes balcony main-floor level, tall windows 6 above 9-paned sashes; listed in 1848 city directory (No. 29) John Dimon; changes to lights around front door, stair annex built on west flank; building belongs to and used by Packer Collegiate Institute.

Schermerhorn Street

LAID OUT by Peter and Abraham Schermerhorn in 1838, the one block on Brooklyn Heights was the original length of Schermerhorn Street. Except for the Court Street end of the block, a single apartment building, and a small private garage, Schermerhorn Street presents a solid block of mid-nineteenth-century brick and brownstone residences, only two of which are slightly less than a hundred years old.

south side

10. 3-storied brick, low pedimented hood over plain recessed doorway; listed in 1849 city directory (No. 1) Sydney Sanderson, merchant; bracketed cornice, door and ironwork end of XIX cent., plate glass.

12. 3-storied; listed in 1858 city directory (No. 3) James Oats, laborer; modern brick facing, battlements at top, lowered doorway "Tudor."

14. 3-storied brownstone, hoods over openings, mansard roof; listed in 1860 city directory (No. 5) J. P. Wallace, merchant; entrance lowered.

18. 3-storied brick; listed in 1848 city directory (No. 7) John M. Read, counsellor; bracketed cornice, other details stripped, entrance lowered, plate-glass windows.

20, 22, 24, 26. 3-storied row houses, continuous brick façade Nos. 22–26 which may also include No. 20, plain recessed doorways, stairs Type B; 1847 city directory lists No. 20 (No. 9) W. H. Davenport, No. 22 (No. 11) S. M. Conant, BA Academy, and No. 26 (No. 15) Dwight Johnson, merchant; No. 24 in 1851 directory (No. 13) J. Warren Rogers; the front wall of No. 20 has been resurfaced and painted; No. 22 has a bracketed cornice; all have later doors, plate-glass windows.

28. 3-storied brick, similar to No. 20 group; listed in 1848 city directory (No. 17) James Dunbar, merchant (Mary Anne Dunbar, widow, listed n[ear] Court in 1847 directory ?); later bracketed cornice, plate glass.

30. 3-storied brick, originally similar to No. 28; listed in 1847 city directory (b[etween] Clinton & Court) John E. Nitchie (No. 19 in 1848 directory); bracketed cornice, entrance lowered, plate glass.

32, 34. 3-storied duplex, continuous brick wall, plain recessed doorways, coupled stairs Type B; No. 32 listed in 1846 city directory (n[ear] Court) G. Roberts (No. 21 in 1849 directory); No. 34 in 1848 city directory

(No. 23) Charles C. Barlling, sailmaker; later overdoor ornaments, plate glass; No. 34 has bracketed cornice, bay window 2nd floor.

36. 3-storied brick; listed in 1848 city directory (No. 25) Austin W. and Charles Otis, merchants; wall stuccoed, entrance lowered.

38. 3-stored brick; listed in 1852 city directory (No. 27) J. B. Hervey, bleacher; stuccoed, entrance lowered.

40. 3-storied brick; listed in 1855 city directory (No. 29) Charles Prox, prof. of music; mansard roof added, plate glass in windows, cement walls flanking entrance stairs.

north side

15. 3-storied brick; listed in 1849 city directory (No. 8) Charles R. Marvin, broker; stripped of details, stuccoed, entrance lowered, plate glass.

17. 3-storied brick; listed in 1849 city directory (No. 10) William N. Peck, merchant; walls stuccoed, entrance lowered, plate glass.

19, 21. 3-storied row houses, continuous brownstone façade, console cornice, cornices on consoles over 1st-story openings (No. 21 only) originally like No. 25; listed in 1856 city directory (No. 12) Paul W. Caesar (also listed as Powell W. Ceser same year), commission merchant, and (No. 14) William R. Sheldon, merchant; concrete railings and fences.

23. 3-storied; listed in 1857 city directory (No. 16) John Dimon; stuccoed, entrance lowered, modern ironwork.

25. 3-storied brownstone; console cornice, hoods over windows, cornice on consoles over doorway; listed in 1857 city directory (No. 18) Peter O'Hara, marble works.

33. 3-storied brick, corniced labels over openings, doorway otherwise plain, stairs Type B; listed in 1850 city directory (No. 24) Lewis F. Mack, merchant; 4th story added with segmented arched windows, cornice, doors later.

37, 39, 41. 3-storied row houses, bracketed cornice; 1852 city directory lists No. 37 (No. 28) D. Goff, Jr., commission merchant, No. 39 (No. 30) Benjamin Carver, ship chandler, and No. 41 (No. 32) Charles Douglas, clerk, and George S. Douglas, accountant; stuccoed; No. 41 has entrance lowered, others concrete and iron railings.

State Street

(Supplementary illustrations nos. 84 and 85)

PERHAPS named after State Street in Manhattan, this southernmost street within the boundaries of Brooklyn Heights first appeared on Ralph Patchen's estate map of 1829, and was physically realized during the following decade. A fair number of houses are indicated on State in the house guides included in the 1840 and 1841 city directories, such as the row between the lower end of Sidney Place and Clinton Street, but, due to irregularities and changes in the numerical system it is sometimes difficult to coordinate listings with buildings. One notes, for instance, that during the late 1850's "No. 58" designated two separate houses on different sides of the street, No. 75 and No. 80 today. The south side of the block between Hicks and Henry streets contained some odd and some even numbers. Undoubtedly there were originally frame boarding houses along this stretch that were replaced by brick houses during the mid 1840's and later.

State Street has not been spoiled by the erection of modern apartment houses, although the flank of a rather large one abuts it at Clinton; but it still remains lined with mid-nineteenth-century dwellings, many of them having suffered hard wear during recent years of service as rooming houses. A movement afoot to reclaim them as private or semiprivate dwellings now has gotten as far as the middle of the block west of Clinton, and, it is hoped, soon will work all the way to Court Street.

south side

68, 70. 4-storied row houses, continuous brick façade, houses on slightly different levels; Gothic Revival hood molds over openings, doorways otherwise plain, cast-iron tracery railings, fence; No. 68 listed in 1850 city directory (No. 46) Charles Shepard, dry goods; No. 70 in 1855 directory (No. 48) John W. Young, importer; both have later bracketed cornices, hood molds stripped except over doorways, modern doors; No. 68 lacks ironwork.

76, 78, 80. 3-storied row houses, continuous brick façade, high basement; Gothic Revival, hood molds over openings, doorways otherwise plain, casement windows, cast-iron tracery railings and fences; 1848 city directory lists No. 76 (n[ear] Hicks) Stephen H. Thayer, counsellor (No. 154 in 1850 directory), also presumably No. 80 (which had the same street number as present-day No. 75), (No. 58) George Burroughs, clerk, J. Field, clerk, James W. Loco, Henry and Theodore Love, and (?) Snow, clerk; No. 78 listed in 1850 directory (No. 56) James O'Connor, merchant (becomes No. 57 in 1858); No. 76 has story added with parapet; No. 78 has later bracketed cornice, plate glass in sash windows; all have later newel posts, hood molds stripped except over doorways.

82. 4-storied brick, rusticated stone basement, bracketed cornice, cornice hood on consoles over entrance, stairs Type B, contemporary fence; listed in 1858 city directory (No. 58) G[ideon] Sanford, cabinet furniture.

84. 4-storied brick, high basement, bracketed cornice, cornice on brackets over doorway; listed in 1856 city directory (No. 59) Lydia B. Robbins, widow of Frederick, boarding house; later concrete railings and fence in front, fire escape.

90. 4-storied brick, 4 bays wide, high basement; Greek Revival, corniced labels over windows, pilastered doorway, stairs Type E, contemporary iron fence; listed in 1848 city directory (No. 30) M. R. Blanchard, boarding house (No. 61, Fidelia Blanchard, in 1850 directory); perhaps indicated in 1845 directory (No. 30) Francis Le Barron, and in 1843 directory (No. 30) Dr. William H. Dudley (number changed to No. 32 in 1844 directory); later doors, plate glass in windows.

92, 96. 3-storied, continuous Flemish-bond brick façade; Greek Revival, corniced labels over windows, recessed pilastered doorways, antapodia flanking entrance stairs; No. 92 listed in 1840 city directory (n[ear] Henry) Mrs. V. Boyd, boarding house (indicated adjacent to H. J. Marquand in 1841 house guide); No. 96 listed in 1841 directory (n[ear] Henry) Henry J. Marquand, jeweler (No. 34 n[ear] Henry in 1847 directory, No. 65 n[ear] Henry in 1850 directory); No. 92 has contemporary iron fence, railing perhaps a little later, plate glass in windows; No. 96 has later door, doorway crudely stuccoed, ironwork modern, fire escape on front, plate glass 2nd and 3rd stories; Edwin Booth stayed here.

120. 3-storied brick, high stone basement, plain recessed doorway, stairs Type B; listed in 1852 city directory (No. 69) Elizabeth Blackwell, widow; plate-glass windows.

122. 3-storied brick, high basement, corniced labels over windows, pilastered doorway, stairs Type B, note Corinthian pilasters flanking original door; listed in 1848 city directory (No. 71) John Pendergast.

124. 4-storied brick, corniced labels over windows; listed in 1845 city directory (No. 73) A. Downs, flour; late XIX cent. cornice, entrance lowered, plate glass.

126. 3-storied brick, Greek Revival, door enframement with "Greek ears" supporting pediment, stairs Type E, corniced labels over windows, contemporary fence; listed in 1842 city directory (n[ear] Henry) Joshua Clibborn, merchant (No. 75 in 1845 directory); door later.

128. 3-storied brick; listed in 1842 city directory (n[ear] Henry) William Maxwell, broker (No. 77 in 1845 directory); later mansard roof, stuccoed, alterations to stairs, plate glass.

130. 3-storied brick, corniced labels over windows; listed in 1846 city directory (No. 79) Alfred Hoyt, merchant; hood cornices over 1st-story openings, later stone and iron railings and fence, plate glass in windows.

132. 4-storied brick; listed in 1847 city directory (No. 81) Charles Stoddard, shipmaster; bracketed cornice, entrance lowered, plate glass.

134, 136, 138, 140. 3-storied row houses, continuous brick façade, high basement; Greek Revival, stone door enframement with "Greek ears," anthemion motif on pediment block above, corniced labels over windows; Nos. 136, 138 listed in 1843 city directory (n[ear] Clinton) G. C. Satterlee (No. 85 in 1845 directory), and H. Huttleson (No. 87 in 1845 directory); Nos. 134, 140 listed in 1845 directory (No. 83) H. C. Beach, merchant, and (No. 89) H. Swift; Nos. 134, 136, 138 have 4th story with bracketed cornices; No. 134 entrance lowered; No. 140 doorway stripped; doors, plate glass and ironwork later.

160, 162. 3-storied row houses, continuous brick façade; Greek Revival, pilastered recessed doorways, steps Type E; listed in 1842 city directory (n[ear] Clinton) Gilbert Beam, cooper (No. 99 in 1846 directory), and (n[ear] Clinton) John Beam, cooper (No. 101 in 1846 directory); doorways modified; door of No. 160 later.

164. 3-storied brick, corniced labels over windows; listed in 1843 city directory (No. 103) William H. Priest, auctioneer; 4th floor added, bracketed cornice, entrance lowered, plate glass in windows, ironwork modern.

174. 3-storied frame; perhaps indicated in 1839 city directory (n[ear] Clinton) John Parton, accountant (south side of State between Clinton and Court in 1840 house guide); listed in 1844 directory (n[ear] Court) James P. Wallace (No. 111 n[ear] Court in 1847 directory); console cornice, entrance lowered, baybuilt 1st story over entrance.

north side

23, 25. 4-storied, continuous brick façade; listed in 1846 city directory (No. 33) Henry Hockhaisst, and (No. 35) Christopher Risley; stores 1st floor, bracketed cornice, plate glass.

27. 4-storied brick; listed in 1848 city directory (No. 37) Mark Brombergh, cap maker; plate glass in windows, store 1st floor.

45, 47. 3-storied brick, bracketed cornice to low-pitched gable in front; No. 45 listed in 1857 city directory (No. 41) Harry H. Beadle, clerk, No. 47 in 1860 directory, William J. Read, printer; store 1st floor.

75. 4-storied brick, contemporary fence; originally had same house number as No. 80 State Street, perhaps listed in 1848 city directory under various names (No. 58) George Burroughs, clerk, J. Field, clerk, James W. Loco, Henry and Theodore Love, (?) Snow, clerk; listed in 1855 directory (c[orner] Garden) Sarah Le Fevre, boarding house (No. 58 in 1856 directory); entrance on Garden Place has later Eastlake details, rear addition, plate glass, fire escape on State Street front.

77, 79, 81. 3-storied row houses, continuous brick façade, Greek Revival, corniced labels over windows, pilastered doorways, stairs Type B; No. 81 listed in 1846 city directory (n[ear] Henry) John M. Pratt (John and James Pratt, paperhangers, No. 64 in 1848 directory); No. 77 in 1848 directory (No. 60) Joseph W. Greene, jeweler; No. 79 in 1849 directory (No. 62) Captain E. Keyes; Nos. 75, 77 have later doors, plate glass in windows; No. 81 has entrance lowered.

83, 85, 87, 89. 3-storied row houses, continuous brick façade, Greek Revival, pilastered doorway (No. 87 only), stairs Type B; 1846 city directory lists No. 83 (n[ear] Henry) James Myers, clerk (No. 66 in 1848 directory), and No. 85 (n[ear] Henry) T. G. Stearns (Thomas G. Stearns, No. 68 in 1848 directory); 1847 directory lists No. 87 (n[ear] Henry) C. M. Davis, widow (Clarisson Davis, No. 70 in 1849 directory), and No. 89 (c[orner] Henry) William P. Dana, merchant (No. 72 in 1848 directory); Nos. 83, 85, 89 have 4th stories added, entrances lowered; Nos. 83, 87 have plate glass in windows.

103, 105, 107. 3-storied row houses, continuous brick façade, high basement, Gothic Revival, drip molds over openings, traceried ironwork railings and fence, balcony also remaining on No. 107, open galleries across back, interesting side door on No. 107 with relief motif after Minard Lafever (perhaps added from another old house); No. 107

47. Nos. 103, 105, 107 State Street.

listed in 1847 city directory (No. 78) Ami Dows, merchant; No. 103 in 1848 directory (n[ear] Henry) James A. Cowing, merchant (No. 74 in 1849 directory); No. 105 in 1849 directory (No. 76) A. C. Hull, physician; windows of No. 103 have been changed.

109, 111, 113, 115, 117. 3-storied row houses having continuous brick façade, high brownstone basement; Greek Revival, pilastered recessed doorways, entrance stairs Type D (urns missing on pedestals), railings distinguished by use of vertical motif incorporating anthemions top and bottom; Nos. 109, 113 retain contemporary fences. 1839 city directory lists No. 109 (c[orner] Henry [Sidney Place?]) George De Peyster, No. 111 (n[ear] Henry) Walter Greenough, commission merchant, No. 115 (n[ear] Clinton) William Waterman, merchant, No. 117 (n[ear] Clinton) (?) Ryder, widow of Wm. I., No. 113 listed in 1840 directory (n[ear] Henry) Azar S. Marvin; key to identification with respective houses furnished by house guide in 1840 directory giving 7 names for dwellings between Sidney Place and Clinton Street; Nos. 115, 117 have later bracketed cornice, all have later doors, No. 117 entrance lowered, Nos. 113, 115 late XIX cent. ironwork, Nos. 109, 115, 117 1st-floor windows enlarged, plate glass.

119. Originally similar to adjacent houses; listed in 1840 city directory (n[ear] Henry [Clinton or Sidney Place?]) Henry Marquand, jeweler; later changes include stone string courses at 2nd- and 3rd-floor window-sill levels, Eastlake details, mansard roof, cupola on top, iron fence and rails, plate-glass windows.

121. 3-storied brick, similar to No. 109 row; unusual entrance stairs with ironwork like its neighbors, Type G, newel posts with urn finials; listed in 1839 city directory (c[orner] Clinton) Alanson Trask, shoe dealer; later bracketed cornice, plate glass in windows, doorway simplified.

141. 3-storied brownstone, high basement, bracketed cornice, hood cornice on consoles over doorway, stairs Type B, contemporary ironwork; listed in 1859 city directory (No. 98) Clinton Colton, merchant.

143. 3-storied brick, high basement, console cornice over plain recessed doorway; presumably referred to in 1841 city directory (n[ear] Clinton) Alfred Hoyt, agent (No. 79 in 1845 city directory); listed in 1853 directory (No. 100) Rodman B. Dawson, counsellor, attorney and Surrogate's clerk, office City Hall; now Islamic Mission to America, doors changed, metalwork, stuccoed fence modern.

145. 3-storied; listed in 1860 city directory (No. 102) Frances H. Atwater; mansard roof, ornate synthetic stone facing.

147, 149. 3-storied brownstones, console cornices, hood cornices on consoles over openings, stairs Type B, contemporary iron fences; listed in 1856 city directory (No. 104) Henry D. Young, grocer, and (No. 106) Robert T. Wilde.

153, 155. 3-storied sandstone, console cornice, arched windows, cornices on brackets over 1st-story openings; No. 155 listed in 1856 city directory (No. 110) J. C. Herman Frost, commission merchant; No. 153 in 1857 directory (No. 108) George E. Archer, storage; No. 153 has mansard roof.

157, 159, 161, 163, 165. 3-storied row houses, continuous brick façade, brick basement; Greek Revival, No. 159 has pilastered doorway (wood), others plain, entrance stairs Type E; three of group indicated in 1841 city directory (n[ear] Court) occupied by Mrs. J. E. Hathaway, Mrs. Mary Penniman, and Edward

Hincken, ship broker; No. 165 listed in 1845 city directory (n[ear] Court) William E. Thorne, clerk (No. 120 in 1847 directory); No. 159 in 1846 directory (n[ear] Court) T. B. White, merchant (No. 114 n[ear] Court in 1847 directory; 1847 directory lists No. 157 (No. 112) Samuel M. Wolfe, and No. 163 (No. 118) Clinton Cotton; No. 161 listed in 1848 directory (No. 116 n[ear] Court) Lefroy Ravenhill; Nos. 157, 159 have bracketed cornice, all have later doors, plate-glass windows.

Supplement of Photographs
by
Edmund V. Gillon, Jr.

48. Jehovah's Witnesses Building, No. 119 Columbia Heights.

49. No. 138 Columbia Heights.

50. Nos. 138–144 Columbia Heights.

51. No. 178 Columbia Heights.

52. No. 157 Columbia Heights.

53. Nos. 111–115 Columbia Heights.

54. Back of Montague Terrace Houses, seen from the Promenade.

55. Entrance to the Esplanade at Pierrepont Place.

56. No. 70 Willow Street.

57. Nos. 108–112 Willow Street.

58. No. 45 Willow Street.

59. Nos. 38, 40 Hicks Street.

60. No. 100 Hicks Street.

61. Nos. 276, 278 Hicks Street.

62. No. 253 Hicks Street.

63. Grace Church, Hicks Street and Grace Court.

64. Nos. 30–34 College Place.

65. No. 21 Garden Place.

66. Nos. 29–43 Garden Place.

67. Nos. 134–138 Henry Street.

68. Nos. 253–257 Henry Street.

69. Atlantic Avenue and Henry Street.

70. Nos. 9–15 Monroe Place.

The trees are bigger now, and there is more vegatation in all the little yards,

71. Saint Charles Borromeo, Sidney Place.

72. No. 51 Sidney Place.

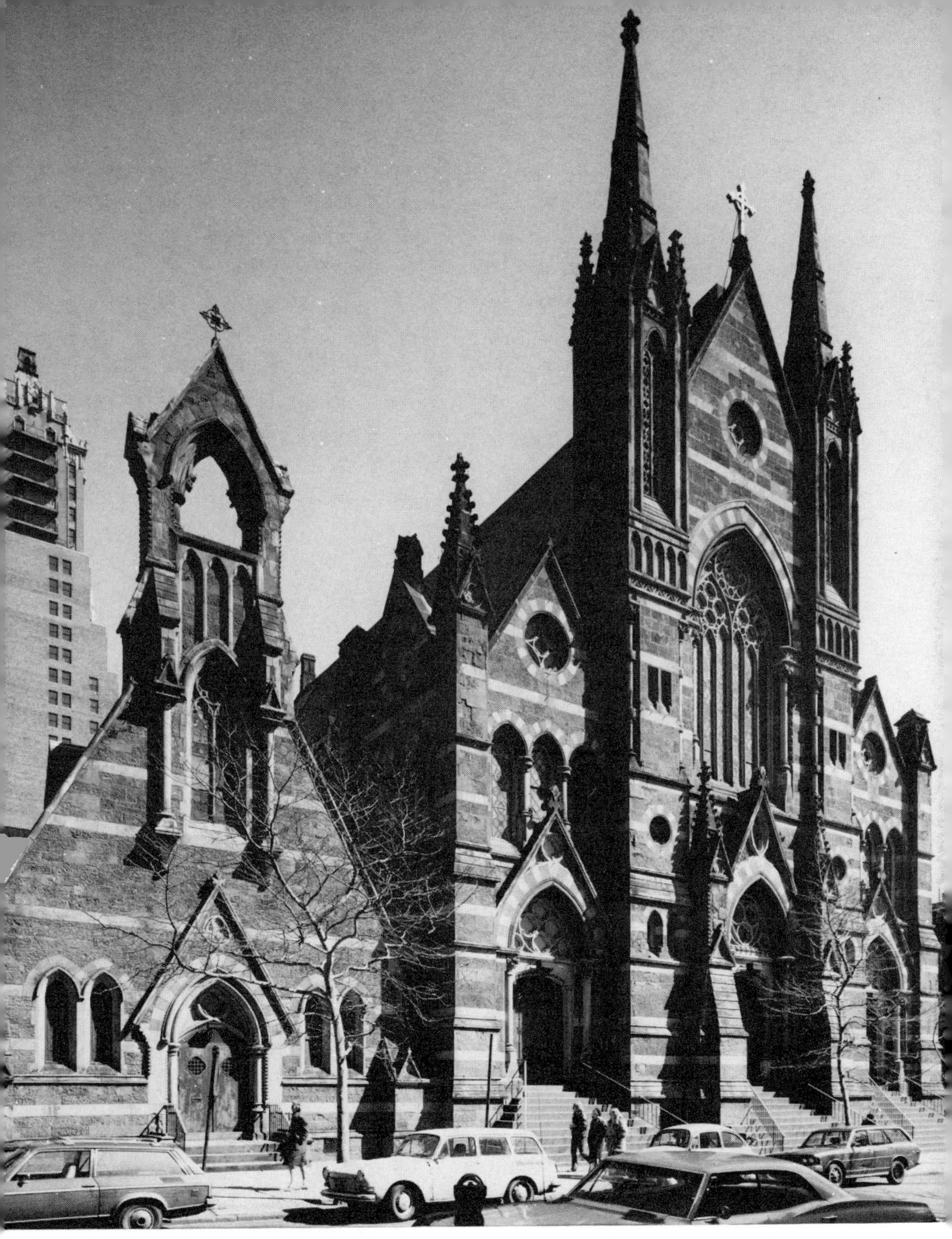

73. Old Saint Anne's Church, Clinton Street at Livingston Street.

74. Nos. 133, 135 Clinton Street.

75. Nos. 153–167 Clinton Street.

76. Nos. 31, 33 Middagh Street.

77. Nos. 22–30 Orange Street.

78. Plymouth Church, Orange Street.

79. Long Island Historical Society, Pierrepont Street at Clinton Street.

around the corner from us

80. No. 124 Remsen Street.

81. Grace Court.

82. No. 4 Grace Court Alley.

83. Nos. 40–44 Joralemon Street.

84. Nos. 35–47 Joralemon Street.

85. Nos. 77, 79 State Street.

86. No. 111 State Street.

87. *Nos. 147–165 State Street.*

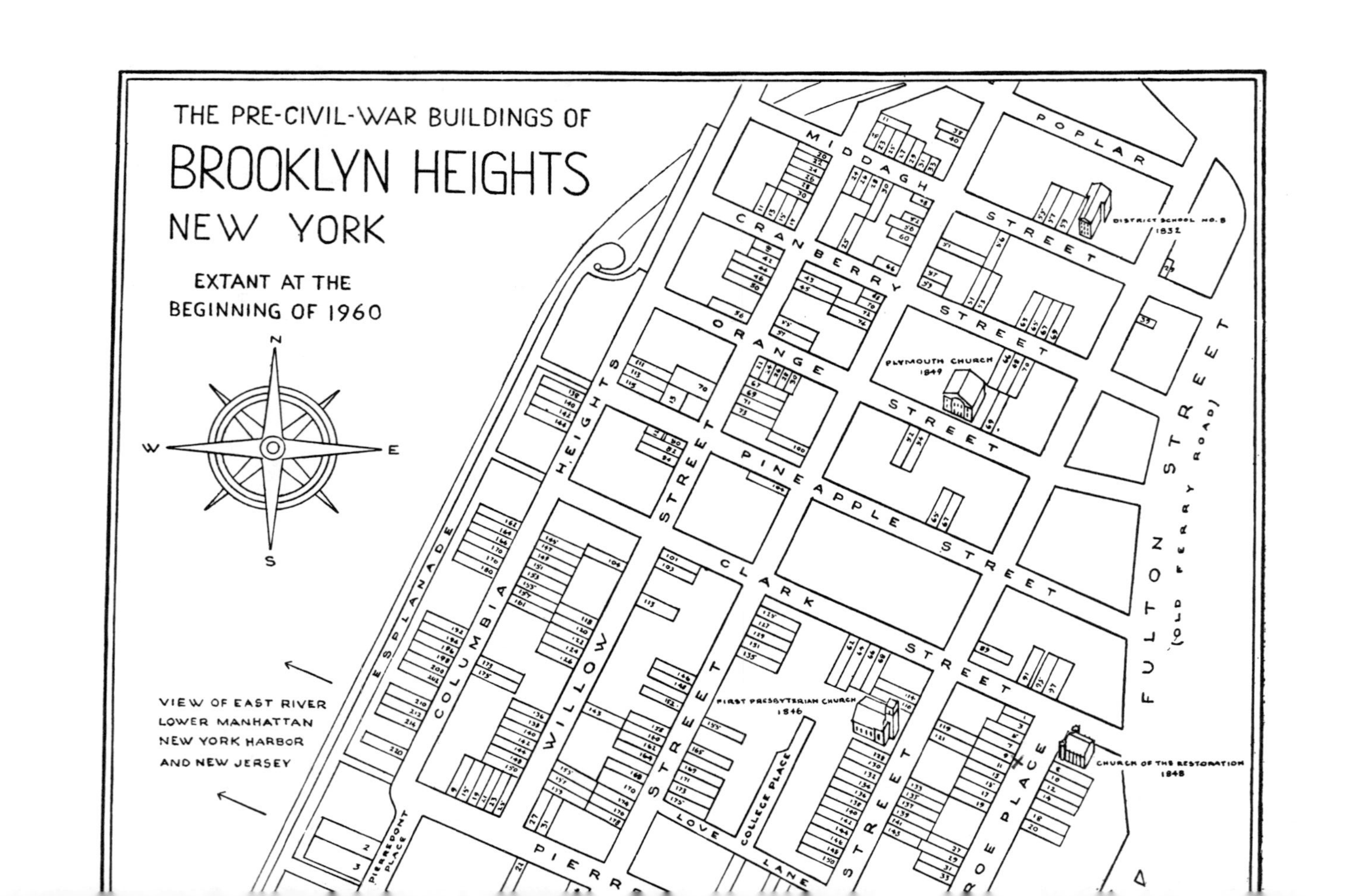

THE PRE-CIVIL-WAR BUILDINGS OF
BROOKLYN HEIGHTS
NEW YORK
EXTANT AT THE
BEGINNING OF 1960
N
E
S
W
VIEW OF EAST RIVER
LOWER MANHATTAN
NEW YORK HARBOR
AND NEW JERSEY
POPLAR
MIDDAGH STREET
CRANBERRY STREET
ORANGE STREET
PINEAPPLE STREET
CLARK STREET
PIERREPONT
FULTON STREET
(OLD FERRY ROAD)
HEIGHTS
WILLOW STREET
COLUMBIA
ESPLANADE
HICKS STREET
MONROE PLACE
COLLEGE PLACE
LOVE LANE
PIERREPONT PLACE
DISTRICT SCHOOL NO. 8
1832
PLYMOUTH CHURCH
1849
FIRST PRESBYTERIAN CHURCH
1846
CHURCH OF THE RESTORATION
1848

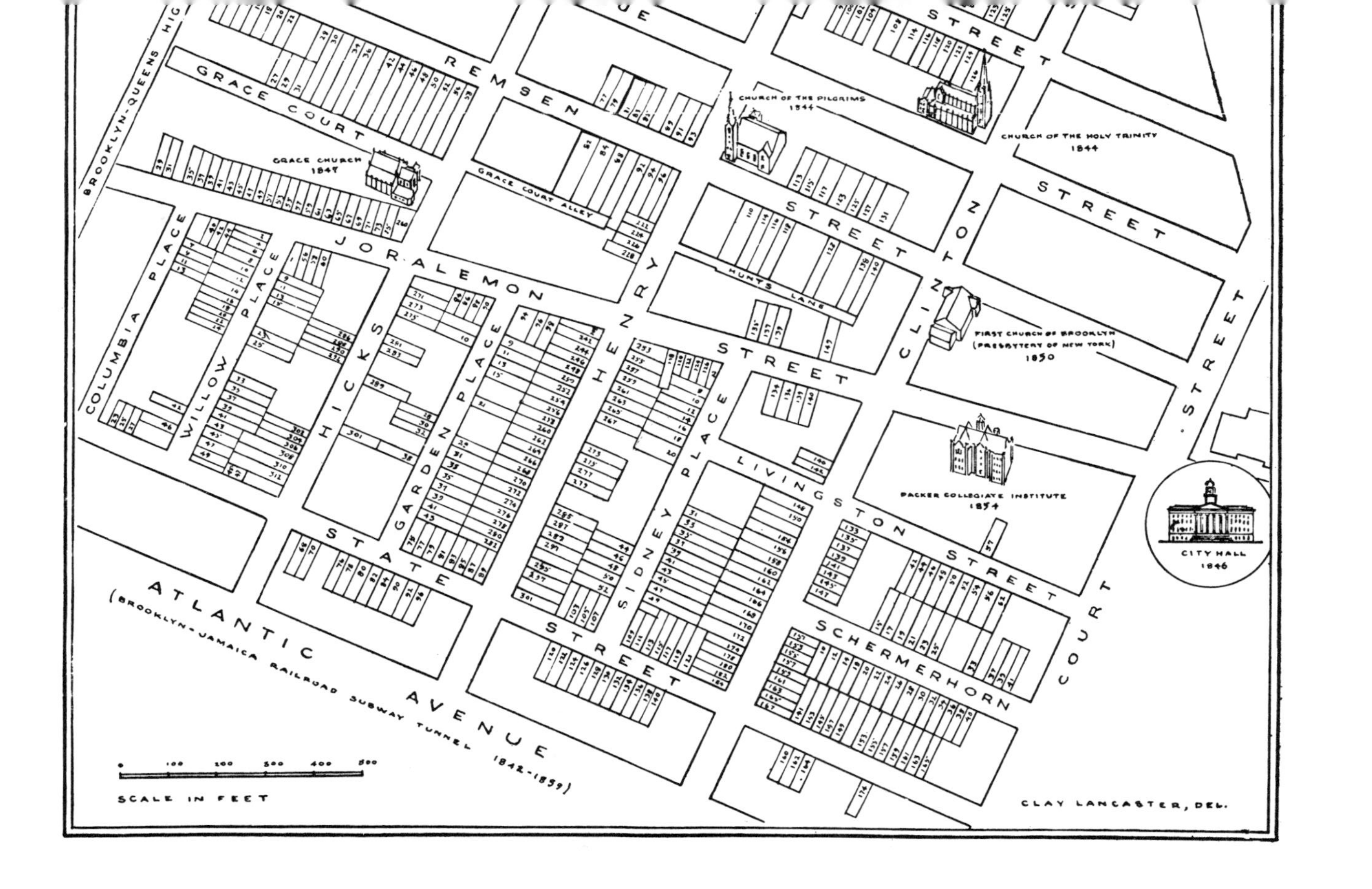

REMSEN
GRACE COURT
BROOKLYN-QUEENS HIG
GRACE CHURCH
1847
GRACE COURT ALLEY
CHURCH OF THE PILGRIMS
1844
CHURCH OF THE HOLY TRINITY
1844
STREET
HUNTS LANE
CLINTON
FIRST CHURCH OF BROOKLYN
(PRESBYTERY OF NEW YORK)
1850
JORALEMON
HENRY
COLUMBIA PLACE
WILLOW PLACE
HICKS
GARDEN PLACE
SIDNEY PLACE
LIVINGSTON
PACKER COLLEGIATE INSTITUTE
1854
CITY HALL
1846
STATE
SCHERMERHORN
COURT
ATLANTIC AVENUE
(BROOKLYN-JAMAICA RAILROAD SUBWAY TUNNEL 1842-1859)
0 100 200 300 400 500
SCALE IN FEET
CLAY LANCASTER, DEL.

Glossary

ABACUS: the square topmost member of a Doric capital

ACANTHUS: a prickly herb, the leaves of which were used by the Greeks for architectural ornaments

ACROTERIA (Greek, pl.): summit or extremity ornaments on pediments

ANTAPODIA (pl.): literally, in front of the basement, projecting cubic forms

ANTHEMION (Greek): flower, the "honeysuckle" motif

ANTIS: see IN ANTIS

ARCH: (Latin *arcus;* arc of a circle) a curved opening composed of wedge-shaped blocks (voussoirs)

ARCHITECTONIC: pertaining to architecture, architectural

ARCHITRAVE: the first or lowest horizontal member of an entablature

ARCHIVOLT: the inner vertical molding around an arch, corresponding to the straight architrave in an entablature

ARCUATED: pertaining to the use of arches

ATTIC: the top story above a main cornice, sometimes confused with the term garret

BALCON-FENÊTRE (French): windows opening onto a balcony, French doors

BALCONY: a projecting platform surrounded by a railing or balustrade

BALUSTRADE: (Latin *balaustium;* a

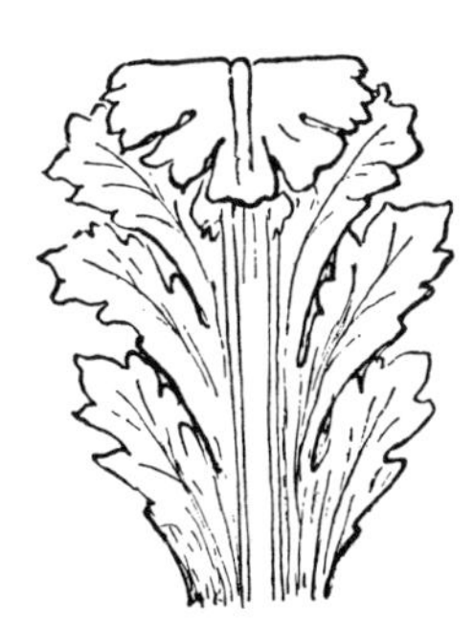

ACANTHUS

ANTHEMION

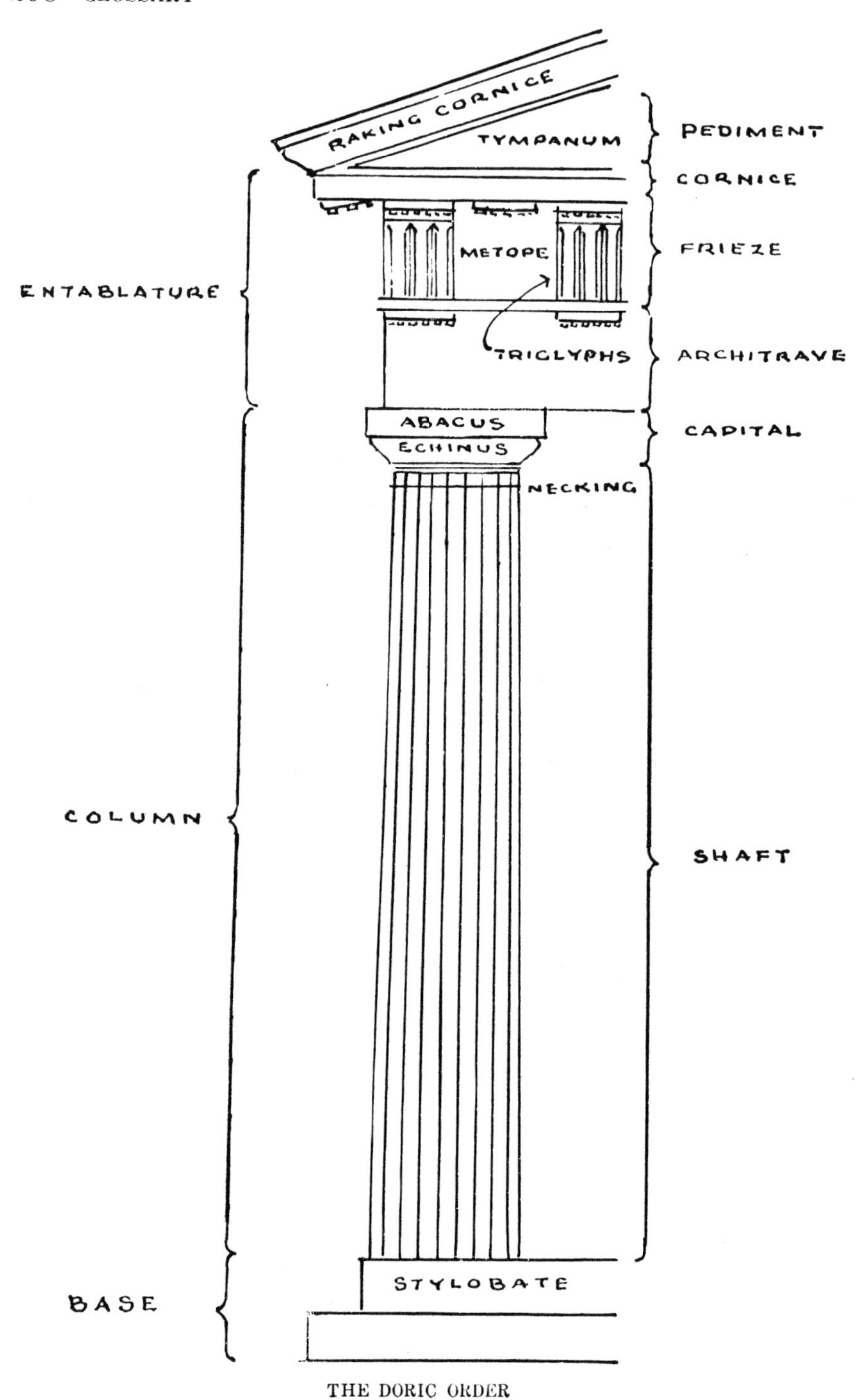

THE DORIC ORDER

pomegranate) a series of upright forms supporting a railing

BASKET URN: an openwork iron form resembling a classic vessel

BASTION: a projection to a fort, usually at the corner, for observing and protecting the flanks

BAY: any architectural unit

BAY WINDOW: a projecting form for admitting light

BEAD-AND-REEL: an ornamental molding made up of small half-spheres alternating with coupled spindle shapes

BEAMED CEILING: ceiling in which beams are exposed to view inside the room

BLIND ARCH: an applied arch, not open through

BLUESTONE: a hard blue-gray stone cut in wide, thin slabs, used for paving

BRACKET: a projecting member to support an overhanging form

BROWNSTONE: a reddish-brown sandstone used in building

CAGE POST: an openwork newel or hollow prism made up of slender iron bars

CAMPANIFORM: bell-shaped

CAPITAL: the head of a column

CASEMENT: a window that swings open on hinges (as opposed to sash window)

CAST IRON: ironwork formed in the melted stage in molds

CHEVRON: a design made up of a series of parallel V-shaped bars

CHIMNEY BREAST: the chimney of a fireplace projecting into a room

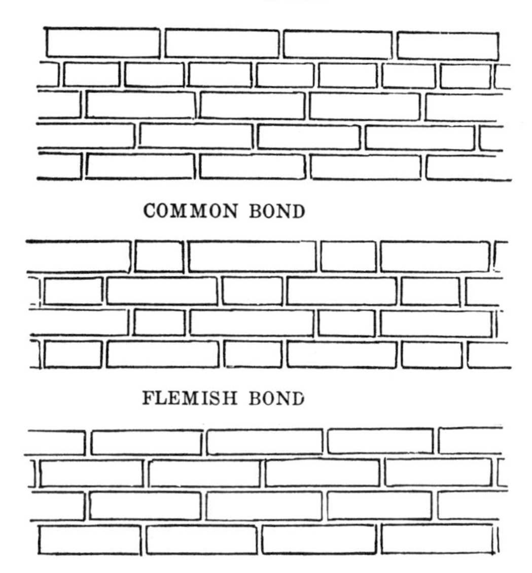

COMMON BOND

FLEMISH BOND

UNBONDED BRICKWORK

CLAPBOARD: an overlapping weatherboard applied horizontally

CLERESTORY: a row of windows high in the wall

COFFERED: having recessed panels

COLONIAL REVIVAL: the imitation of the Colonial and Federal styles that flourished during the late nineteenth and early twentieth centuries

COLONNETTES: small, slender columns

COLOSSAL ORDER: the use of columns several stories high

COLUMN: a classic support having base, shaft, and capital

COMMON BOND: brickwork composed of several layers of bricks laid sidewise (stretchers) bonded by a row laid endwise (headers), repeated in regular succession

CONSOLE: a bracket of classic form, usually scrolled at top and bottom

CONTINUOUS BRICKWORK: brickwork in which a brick wall carries through from one building to the next, signifying their simultaneous construction

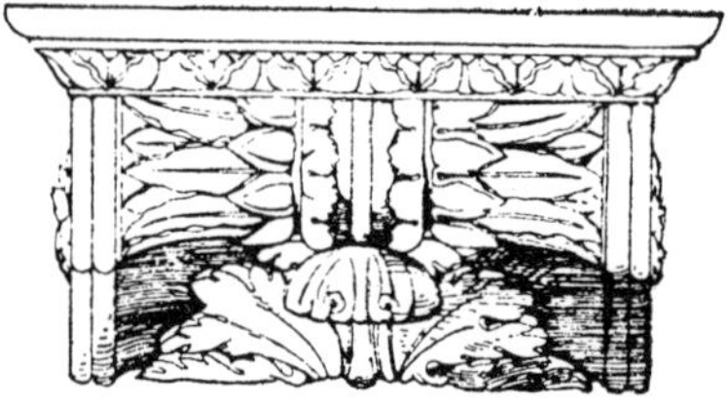

CONSOLE (ROMAN)

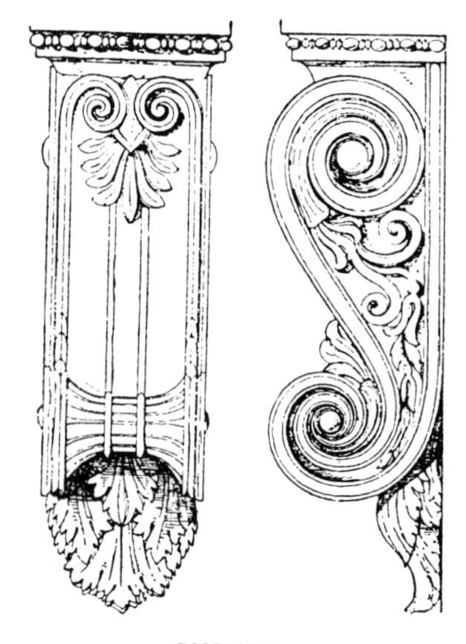

CONSOLE

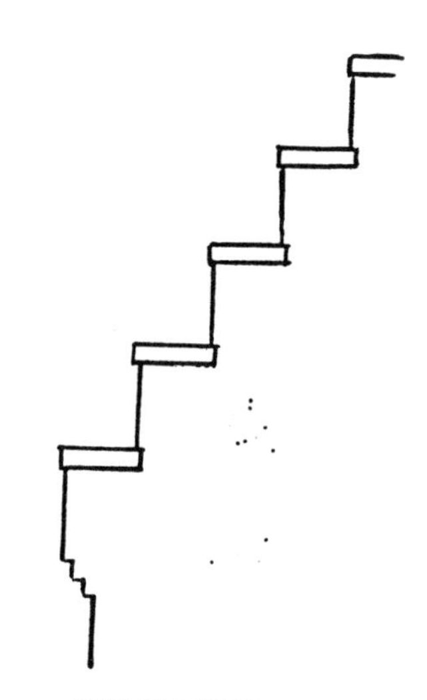

CORBIE STEPS

CORBIE-STEPPED: literally crow-stepped, a parapet having a saw-tooth outline

CORINTHIAN: the order of classic architecture distinguished by campaniform capitals ornamented with acanthus leaves

CORNICE: the topmost, projecting member of an entablature, sometimes used alone

CORNICED LABEL: a term used in this book to signify a plain stone lintel flush with the wall plane having a molding across the top

CORNUCOPIA: horn of plenty

COSMATESQUE: floor inlaid with small pieces of stone or tile

COUPLED COLUMNS: columns grouped in pairs

COUPLED WINDOWS: a pair of windows separated only by a stanchion

CRESTING: an openwork ornament along a horizontal edge or ridge

CROCKET: (French *croc*; a hook) an ornament often resembling foliage spaced along a gothic gable or spire

CURB ROOF: a gabled roof having a double slope

DISTYLE: a portico or porch having two columns

DORIC: the common Greek order, distinguished by a heavy column, without base, a channeled shaft,

GABLE WITH CROCKETS

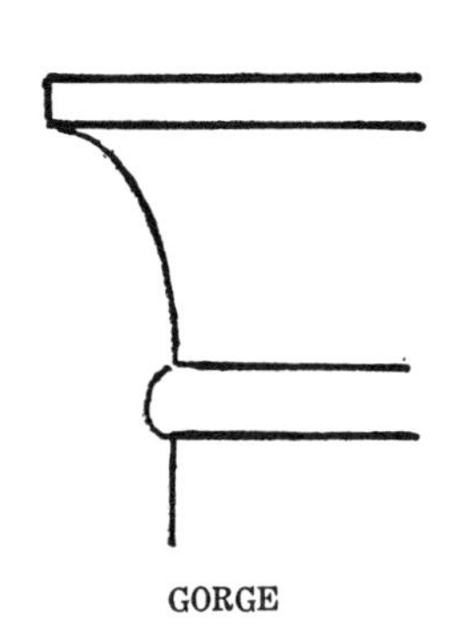
GORGE

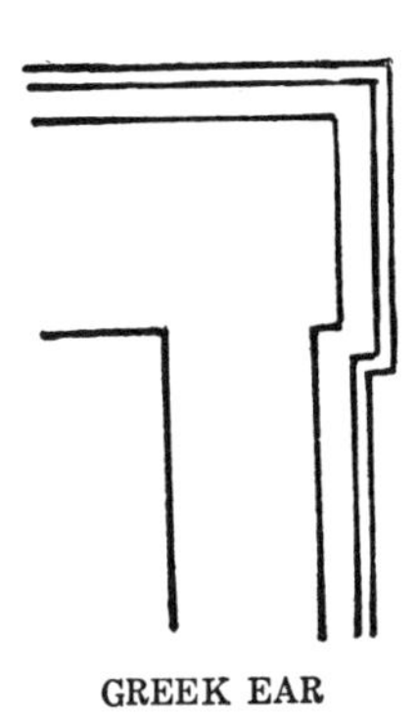
GREEK EAR

and a capital made up of an echinus and square abacus

DORMER: a window form that projects through a sloping roof

DRIP MOLD: a hood mold with pendant sides

DUPLEX: double, used in connection with two houses forming inverted halves of a single composition

EASTLAKE: the manner of the English designer Sir Charles Locke Eastlake (1836–1906); see section on "Queen Anne" style

ECHINUS: the cushion form supporting the square abacus of a Doric column

ENFRAMEMENT: a frame, or molding encircling an opening

ENTABLATURE: the horizontal part of an architectural order, supported on columns, composed of architrave, frieze, and cornice

FAÇADE: the front of a building

FANLIGHT: a half-circular of half-elliptical window, usually over a door

FEDERAL: the early-nineteenth-century architectural style

FINIAL: a crowning ornament, as on a post

FLANK: the side of a building

FLEMISH BOND: a type of brickwork composed of alternating bricks laid sidewise (stretchers) and endwise (headers), creating a checkerboard-like pattern

FRET: an ornamental network of geometric lines

FRIEZE: the second member of an entablature, in classic architecture usually containing relief carvings

GABLE: the triangular shape at the end of a building made by a sloping roof

GALLERY: a long narrow room or covered porch

GARGOYLE: a projecting waterspout, usually carved in the form of a grotesque beast

GARRET: the top story under the slope of a roof

GORGE: a concave horizontal molding that springs upward and outward from a wall

GOTHIC: the later medieval style in Europe, distinguished by pointed arches

GOTHIC REVIVAL: in America the nineteenth-century style inspired by the European gothic

"GREEK EARS": projections near the top of enframements to doors of the Greek Revival period

PALLADIAN WINDOW

GREEK REVIVAL: the style inspired by antique Greek buildings, employed in America during the first six decades of the nineteenth century

GUILLOCHE: an ornament composed of interlaced curvilinear bands

HOOD: a projection at the top of an opening to shed rainwater

IN ANTIS: literally, between antae (piers), said of columns supporting the wall in a recessed doorway

IONIC: the classic order distinguished by volutes on the capital

ITALIANATE: in the Italian manner, a mid-nineteenth-century architectural style

JAMB: an upright forming the side of an opening

KEYSTONE: the centermost voussoir of an arch, often given some special architectural treatment

LABEL: a lintel; see CORNICED LABEL

LANCET ARCH: an acutely pointed opening

LEADED GLASS: window glass held in place by lead muntins

LINTEL: the horizontal member bridging two vertical supports

LOUVERS (pl.): sloping slats placed horizontally in an opening to exclude rain or direct sunlight but allow the passage of air

LUNETTE: a half-moon window, or wall space beneath an arch or vault

MANSARD: a roof with steep lower slopes and flatter upper portion on all four sides, named after the seventeenth-century French architect Jules Hardouin Mansard, used on Brooklyn Heights during last half of nineteenth century

MEANDER: an endless fret design

MOLDING: a long strip of material having a definite profile used for decorative purposes

MULLION: a supporting pier between window lights (usually of stone or wood)

MUNTIN: a slender window bar (usually of wood or lead)

NEO-CLASSIC: literally, new-classic; the late-nineteenth-century revival of the classic

NEWEL POST: the main post at the base of a stair railing

NOSING: the molding across the top of the riser of a step

OBELISK: a tall tapering square form capped by a pyramid, an ancient Egyptian monument

ORDER: a type of column and entablature combination, viewed as the

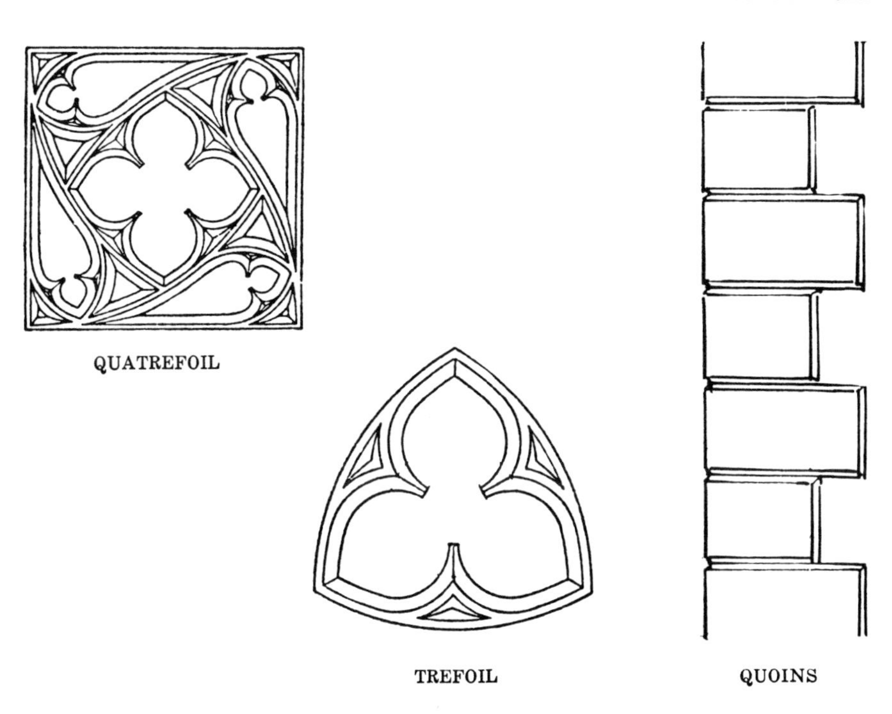

QUATREFOIL

TREFOIL

QUOINS

unit of a style; the Greeks used three orders, the Doric, Ionic, and Corinthian

PALLADIAN MOTIF: an opening of three lights, the centermost being arched

PARAPET: a wall section rising above a roof

PARGETING: ornamental plaster reliefs

PARQUETRY: wood inlaid in patterns

PAVILION: a small building, or individual mass or wing of a building of complex form

PEDESTAL: a base or small foundation, usually a single block of stone having moldings at top and bottom

PEDIMENT: the triangular form of a classic gable

PERPENDICULAR PERIOD: the late gothic style in England (fifteenth century) in which upright lines predominate

PIER: an upright support

PILASTER: a flat upright member applied to a wall, treated like a column with base, shaft and capital

PINNACLE: an ornamental peak or small spire

PLATE GLASS: rolled sheet glass, post Civil War period

PORTE-COCHÈRE: a carriage entrance

PORTICO: a classic porch

POST: a free-standing support

QUATREFOIL: a four-lobed gothic ornament (usually open)

"QUEEN ANNE": a late-nineteenth-century style inspired by the early English Renaissance

QUOINS: projecting end blocks used decoratively

RECESSED DOORWAY: an entrance placed behind the plane of the front wall, the opening usually enframed by an entablature and

TRACERY

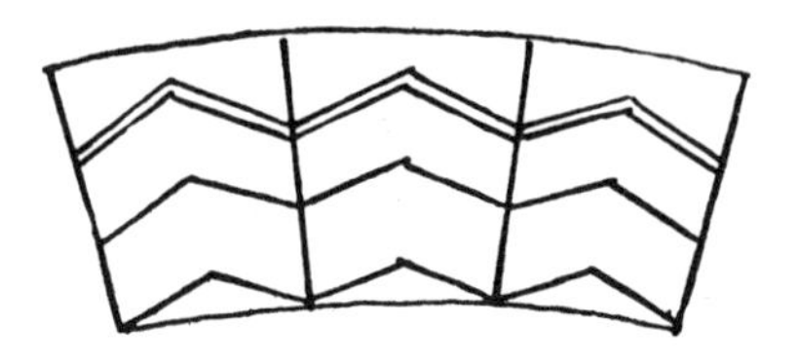
CHEVRON MOULDING ON VOUSSOIRS OF ARCH

pilasters or moldings with "Greek ears" at the upper corners

RENAISSANCE: literally, the rebirth, i.e. the rebirth of classical culture following the medieval period

RENAISSANCE REVIVAL: the imitation of the Renaissance style during the middle and late nineteenth century

RISER: the front plane of a step

ROMANESQUE: the early medieval style, distinguished by heavy walls and round-headed windows

ROMANESQUE REVIVAL: the mid- to late-nineteenth-century style based upon the European Romanesque

ROSETTE: a stylized rose shape

RUSKINIAN: Venetian Gothic, the style advocated by the English critic John Ruskin (1819–1900), popular in America during the late 1860's

RUSTIC: in its natural state, not shaped by man

RUSTICATION: stonework in which the blocks have beveled or rabbeted edges making the joints more conspicuous

SARACENIC: the Near Eastern style, distinguished by horseshoe arches, domes, and interlaced decorations

SASH: the framing in which panes of glass are set in windows, the type that raises and lowers

SCROLL PEDIMENT: a pediment in which the raking cornices end in volutes instead of rising to a peak

SEGMENTED ARCH: an arch that is less than half of a circle or ellipse, meeting the jambs in angles; see ARCH

SHINGLE: a thin slab of wood or other material for covering roofs

SPANDREL: the triangular space between the curve of an arch and its rectangular enframement

SPIRE: a slender tapering roof surmounting a tower

STAIRHALL: a passage containing steps to other floors

STANCHION: a vertical support, as in a window

"STICK STYLE": the late-nineteenth-century manner of building in wood

STUCCO: a type of cement used to form a hard covering for exterior walls

SYNTHETIC STONE: the use of stucco to resemble stonework

TERRACOTTA: a hard baked clayware used for external architectural embellishment, usually a dark red color

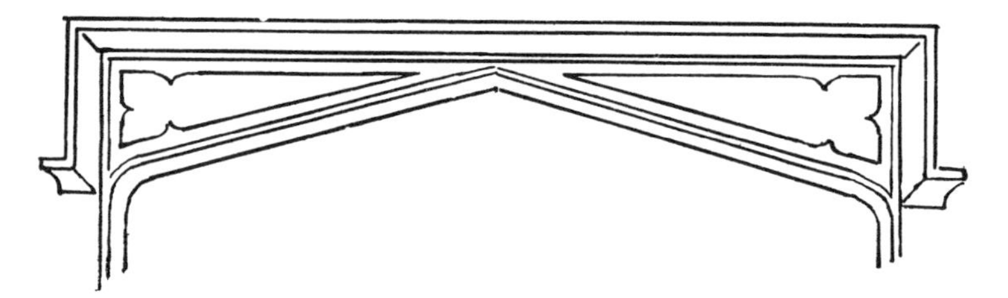

TUDOR ARCH WITH HOOD MOULD AND TREFOIL SPANDRELS

TRACERY: the open patternwork in a gothic window

TRANSOM: a window over a door

TRANSVERSE HALL: a passage that cuts through a house from front to back

TREAD: the horizontal member of a step

TREFOIL: a three-lobed ornamental motif (gothic)

TRIPLE WINDOW: a window of three lights, the centermost usually three times the width of the side lights

TRUNCATED: the form left after part has been removed

TUDOR ARCH: a low-pitched pointed arch, theoretically four-centered

TURRET: a small tower, usually at the angle of a larger structure

TUSCAN: the Roman Doric style (the column is more slender than in the Greek, and has a base and plain shaft)

TYMPANUM: the space enclosed by an arch or pediment

UNBONDED: a masonry wall having all-stretcher (sidewise) bricks exposed

VENETIAN GOTHIC: the late medieval style used in Venice, distinguished by banded stonework in two tones

VESTIBULE: a small outer room or entrance hall

VOID PATTERN: the empty or negative spaces in a design

VOLUTE: a spiral form, as in an Ionic capital

VOUSSOIRS: the wedge-shaped stones composing an arch

References

BROOKLYN CITY DIRECTORIES CONSULTED (year and publisher)

1822–26 and 1829, Alden Spooner
1830–31, Lewis Nichols
1832, William Bigelow
1833, Lewis Nichols & —— Delaree
1834, Alden Spooner and William Bigelow
1835–36, Lewis Nichols
1837–38, A. G. Stevens & William H. Marschalk
1839, Henry L. Ogden
1840, T. & J. W. Leslie & W. F. Chichester
1841, Thomas Leslie & John W. Leslie
1842, James E. & John K. Webb & William J. Hearne
1843, Thomas Leslie, Henry R. & William J. Hearne
1844, Henry R. & William J. Hearne & Edwin Van Nostrand
1845, Henry R. & William J. Hearne
1846, William J. Hearne & Edwin Van Nostrand
1847, William J. Hearne & James E. Webb
1848–54, Henry R. & William J. Hearne
1855, William H. Smith
1856, G. Clark Henderson
1857–61, J. Lain

BROOKLYN AND BROOKLYN HEIGHTS

Henry R. Stiles, *A History of the City of Brooklyn*, 3 vols., Brooklyn, 1867–70

Maud Esther Dilliard, *Old Dutch Houses of Brooklyn*, New York, 1945

James H. Callender, *Yesterdays on Brooklyn Heights*, New York, 1927

B. Meredith Langstaff, *Brooklyn Heights, Yesterday, Today, Tomorrow*, Brooklyn, 1937

Brooklyn Trust Company, *Rambles About Historic Brooklyn*, Brooklyn, 1916

The Brooklyn Savings Bank, *Old Brooklyn Heights*, New York, 1927

Henry Hope Reed, Jr., *Brooklyn Heights, A Walking Tour* (mimeographed guide), New York, 1957

Henry Hope Reed, Jr. & John Barrington Bayley, *Classical Brooklyn: Its Architecture and Sculpture,* mimeographed catalogue for an exhibition at the Long Island Historical Society, Brooklyn, 1956

THE FEDERAL STYLE

Sidney Fiske Kimball, *Domestic Architecture of the American Colonies and of the Early Republic,* New York, 1922 ***(Dover Reprint)***

THE GREEK REVIVAL STYLE

Talbot F. Hamlin, *Greek Revival Architecture in America,* Oxford, 1944 ***(Dover Reprint)***

Howard Major, *The Domestic Architecture of the Early American Republic: The Greek Revival,* Philadelphia, 1926

Minard Lafever, *The Young Builder's General Instructor,* Newark, 1829

Minard Lafever, *The Modern Builder's Guide,* New York, 1833 ***(Dover Reprint)***

Minard Lafever, *The Beauties of Modern Architecture,* New York, 1835

THE GOTHIC REVIVAL STYLE

Kenneth Clark, *The Gothic Revival,* London, 1928

Agnes Eleanor Addison, *Romanticism and the Gothic Revival,* Philadelphia, 1938

Everard Miller Upjohn, *Richard Upjohn, Architect and Churchman,* New York, 1939

Andrew Jackson Downing, *The Architecture of Country Houses,* New York, 1850 ***(Dover Reprint)***

Minard Lafever, *The Architectural Instructor,* New York, 1856

THE ROMANESQUE REVIVAL STYLE

Carroll L. V. Meeks, "Romanesque Before Richardson in the United States," *The Art Bulletin,* March, 1953, pp. [17]–33

Henry-Russell Hitchcock, *The Architecture of H. H. Richardson and His Times,* New York, 1936

THE ITALIANATE STYLE AND RENAISSANCE REVIVAL

Carroll L. V. Meeks, "Henry Austin and the Italian Villa," *The Art Bulletin,* June, 1948, pp. 145–49

Clay Lancaster, "Italianism in American Architecture Before 1860," *American Quarterly,* Summer, 1952, pp. 127–48

RUSKINIAN OR VENETIAN-GOTHIC STYLE

John Ruskin, *The Seven Lamps of Architecture,* New York, 1849
John Ruskin, *The Stones of Venice,* New York, 1851

LATE-NINETEENTH-CENTURY AMERICAN ARCHITECTURE

Henry Van Brunt, "Architecture at the World's Columbian Exposition," *Century,* May, 1892, pp. 81–99
John J. Flinn, *Official Guide to the World's Columbian Exposition in the City of Chicago . . . ,* Chicago, *ca.* 1893
Architectural Book Publishing Company, *A Monograph of the Work of McKim, Mead & White,* New York, *ca.* 1914–15
Carroll L. V. Meeks, "Picturesque Eclecticism," *The Art Bulletin,* September, 1950, pp. 226–35
Vincent J. Scully, Jr., *The Shingle Style,* New Haven, 1955

Index